LETTING Go,
HANGING On

Jo Barbara —

John L. Braden, osfs

LETTING Go, HANGING On

A Guide for the Spiritual Journey

JOHN L. GRADEN

Foreword by Wendy M. Wright

Paulist Press
New York / Mahwah, NJ

Cover image by Shutterstock.com
Cover and book design by Sharyn Banks

Library of Congress Cataloging-in-Publication Data

Graden, John (Oblate priest)
    Letting go, hanging on : a guide for the spiritual journey / John L. Graden; foreword by Wendy M. Wright.
        pages cm
    Includes bibliographical references.
    ISBN 978-0-8091-4883-7 (pbk. : alk. paper) — ISBN 978-1-58768-372-5 (e book)
    1. Spiritual life—Catholic Church. 2. Francis, de Sales, Saint, 1567–1622. 3. Chantal, Jeanne-Françoise de, Saint, 1572–1641. I. Title.
    BX2350.3.G69 2015
    248.4`82—dc23

2014049709

ISBN 978-0-8091-4883-7 (paperback)
ISBN 978-1-58768-372-5 (e-book)

Published by Paulist Press
997 Macarthur Boulevard
Mahwah, New Jersey 07430

www.paulistpress.com

Printed and bound in the
United States of America

For all of you,
whom I affectionately held in heart and mind
as I wrote this book.

Contents

ACKNOWLEDGMENTS ix

FOREWORD BY WENDY M. WRIGHT.................................xi

ABBREVIATIONS xv

Introduction 1

Chapter 1: Attachment 7

Chapter 2: Possessions 15

Chapter 3: It's All about Me! 24

Chapter 4: Who Do I Think I Am? 34

Chapter 5: The Concept of God 43

Chapter 6: Success, Failure, and the Need to Be Right ..53

Chapter 7: Friendships, Relationships, and Forgiveness..62

Chapter 8: The Gift of Sexuality 74

Chapter 9: Prayer 87

Chapter 10: Consolation and Hope 101

Chapter 11: **Spirituality of the Present Moment** 110

Chapter 12: **Holy Indifference** 122

Appendix I: **St. Francis (François) de Sales (1567–1622)** 128

Appendix II: **St. Jeanne-Françoise (Jane) Frémyot de Chantal (1572–1641)** 130

Appendix III: **Salesian Spirituality**..................132

Select Bibliography 135

Acknowledgments

In addition to the family that brought me into the world and were my first teachers, and the many Oblates of St. Francis de Sales who have helped me to be who I am today, I would like especially to thank those men and women who were my confidants, counselors, and inspiration over many years, many of whom were Oblate priests themselves.

In my early years at St. Francis de Sales Parish in Toledo, it was Fred Hug and Jerry Neidermeier, confessors, and Sr. Cassilda who taught me about the Sacred Heart.

At St. Francis de Sales High School, Lou Komorowski and Eugene Schings, both science teachers, piqued my interest in science and could lend a great ear as well. George Shugrue, the principal, and Ed Zapletal, the band director, always believed in me.

As a young Oblate, I was enriched by Al Gaffigan and Tom Walsh, Tom McHugh, Dominic Finn, Jim Boston, Joe Power, Terry Forestell, and Jim Cryan. As an adult coping with many issues of letting go and hanging on, several lent their ears and hearts to me: Paul Francis, George Freemesser, Jim Richards, Andre Auw, Kevin Ricker, Mary Morgillo, Jim Kantner, Fran Therese Woznicki, MaryAnn Longo, Ray Fisher, Kevin Anderson, Hy Kisin, Ceil Cosgrove, and Michael Caballero. Of course, I am still here because of the generous skills of numerous medical personnel who have saved my life over and over again.

I say particular thanks to Lisa Biedenbach and Jeanne Hunt, whose prodding led to the writing of this book, and to Paul

McMahon, the editor, who made sense out of my thoughts and writings. Behind all this support is the Lord who gave me St. Francis de Sales as the greatest mentor, and all the incredible men and women I have had the opportunity to share with, sing to, and laugh together with in parish missions and confessions over the last thirty-nine years. They have enabled me more than they will ever know.

Foreword

"Ah, so sweet, so flowery. Good for beginnings I guess."

This was the opinion offered to me long ago by a venerable Belgian Cistercian monk on the occasion of my having informed him that the subject of my doctoral studies was the writings of the seventeenth-century French-speaking Savoyard bishop and spiritual author Francis de Sales. With all due respect to my conversation partner, himself a scholar of a little known medieval ascetic and visionary, I would, after three decades of considering de Sales's spiritual legacy, have to politely if firmly disagree with his assessment. Accessible: yes. This is utterly true of the writings of Francis de Sales. Inviting to those just launched on the spiritual journey: yes. Attractive, even beautiful: yes. In this, my Cistercian colleague, if this is what he meant in his allusion to "sweet and flowery," was correct. However, if by "good for beginners" he meant that such a lovely vision was merely an entry-level spiritual approach destined to be discarded when moving into more rigorous spiritual realms, he was wrong. Can the Savoyard be easily dismissed by mature pilgrims of the Christian way? No.

Salesian spirituality, that school of Catholic Christian wisdom founded by Francis de Sales and his friend and collaborator, Jane de Chantal, has been described as inspired common sense. With a sound grasp of the ways that human beings operate both for good and ill (what we would today call psychology) coupled with a deep and hard-won knowledge of the spiritual practices that facilitate maturation, these two reached out to their contemporaries to share a unique perspective on Christian discipleship. They shared a vision of an interconnected world of divine and human hearts conjoined by the heart of Jesus who invites all to "[come] and learn from me; for I am gentle and humble in heart" (Matt 11:29). This vision was persuasive to women and men who longed to live authentically in the early modern era. The vision continues to compel like-minded seekers today.

Of the two founders, it is Francis who is best known and whose popular writings give twenty-first century pilgrims access to that vision of a world of hearts. In his day, the bishop was indefatigable: beyond the demanding duties of his episcopal office, he preached, offered spiritual guidance, corresponded, and authored a number of manuscripts meant to edify his pastoral charges. His most famous works are *Introduction to the Devout Life*, written primarily for the many laywomen who consulted him about Christian living in the midst of their daily responsibilities, and *Treatise on the Love of God*, a work of pastoral theology that explored the relationship between the divine and human love relationship.

Francis reached out not only to persons who had vowed to live a life set apart: priests and those in religious orders. He reached out to women and men in all life circumstances: married, single, economically advantaged and disadvantaged, well-educated and nominally so, employers and employees, housewives and merchants, public leaders and private citizens. He reached out to any person whose desire prompted him or her to search for the source of all love.

It was to these that he addressed himself in language that was graceful and grace-filled. He laced his prose with memorable stories, metaphors, and allusions in order to bring the most subtle of spiritual teachings to life. Through them, de Sales's readers were offered a mirror into which they could gaze and see themselves reflected. He utilized images familiar to his readers: as gentlewomen were accustomed to gathering bouquets of flowers to carry with them throughout the day for their scent, he encouraged readers to gather daily "spiritual nosegays" plucked from their daily prayers to foster awareness of God's presence. He counseled God's children to attend to the behavior of little chicks that find safety under the mother hens' wings and to find peace by likewise seeking the shelter of their heavenly Father's heart. His images were current and commonsensical and at the same time, if plumbed, capable of coaxing the reader out of complacency, of turning someone inside out so that he or she might be truly born anew.

De Sales wrote for his era, but his insights, encoded in those images, have stood the test of time. They rang true two hundred years after his death when nineteenth-century Europe witnessed what has been termed a "Salesian Pentecost." A startling number of religious communities and associations—among them the Salesians of Don Bosco who work with marginalized youth, and the men's and women's teaching communities of the Oblates of St. Francis de Sales, founded by Blessed Louis Brisson—sprang up inspired by the vision that de Sales shared. Each of these new groups explored Salesian spirituality in a different way, finding contemporary images to express core spiritual meanings. In the same manner, these insights continue to ring true in the twenty-first century. Fr. John Graden, an Oblate of Saint Francis de Sales, steeped in the saint's teachings, brings those insights alive again in *Letting Go, Hanging On*. Using his own homey, accessible stories to make the same commonsense yet inspired points, Fr. Graden speaks in an identifiably Salesian idiom that is inviting and accessible to readers today.

Salesian spirituality may be saturated with the language of love: God's dynamic, desirous love of creatures and the human desire for God. However, at the core of the vision of conjoined hearts is the heart of Jesus, the heart of One who died of and for love, a Crucified Heart. To "live Jesus," to allow one's own heart to be transformed into a gentle, humble heart, requires discipline, a letting go of those attachments that bind and constrict the heart. In this slim volume, Fr. Graden offers the warm Salesian message: you are a beloved child of God created to love and be loved. But he knows, as did de Sales, that the human heart must be emptied of the burdens it has accumulated, its obsessive self-preoccupations, fears, and ill-directed desires, in order to be free to truly love. This book is about such an opened heart. It is about self-reflection, about discerning the unnecessary and obstructive clutter with which we have filled our lives and hearts and figuring out which attachments are good and true and which are false.

As my Belgian monk seemed to think, Salesian spirituality may indeed beckon beginners onto the pilgrim path. But it also continues to serve the seasoned traveler well. In Fr. John Graden, both novice and long-time practitioner will discover a sure contemporary guide.

Abbreviations

The sources for the multiple quotes from St. Francis de Sales and St. Jane de Chantal are identified using three capital letters as listed below, followed by the section or the page in that particular source.

AVAILABILITY OF SOURCES

D: DeSales Resources and Ministries Lending Library

D-S: Available for purchase from DeSales Resources and Ministries

T: Trexler Library, DeSales University

FREQUENTLY CITED SOURCES

CJC: Jane de Chantal, St. *Her Exhortations, Conferences and Instructions*. Translated by the Visitandines of Bristol, England in 1888 from the French edition printed in Paris in 1875. Revised. Westminster, MD: Newman Bookshop, 1947. (D)

IDL: Francis de Sales, St. *The Introduction to the Devout Life*. Translated and edited by John K. Ryan. New York: Doubleday Image Books, 1950. (D-S)

LSD: Francis de Sales, St. and St. Jane de Chantal. *Letters of Spiritual Direction*. Translated by Perenne Marie Thibert. Selected and introduced by Wendy M. Wright and Joseph F. Power, OSFS. New York: Paulist Press, 1988. (D-S)

LST: Francis de Sales, St. *Selected Letters*. Translated by Elisabeth Stopp. New York: Harper and Brothers, 1960. (D) (D-S) (T)

NJB: Bowden, Nancy Jane. "'Ma Très Chère Fille': The Spirituality of François de Sales and Jeanne de Chantal and the Enablement of Women." Dissertation for University of Washington, 1995. (D) (T)

SNL: Luce, Clare Boothe. *Saints for Now*. New York: Sheed and Ward, 1952. (T)

SPC: Francis de Sales, St. *Spiritual Conferences*. Translated from the Annecy text of 1895 under the supervision of Rev. Henry Mackey, OSB. London: Burns and Oates, 1923. (D)

TLG: Francis de Sales, St. *Treatise on the Love of God*. Translated by John K. Ryan with an introduction and notes by John K. Ryan. 2 vols. Stella Niagara, NY: DeSales Resource Center, 2007. (D) (D-S) (T)

Introduction

St. Francis de Sales is probably the first great doctor of the spirit and director of the soul to bring to light the connection between holiness and humor. For he saw that self-humor, the gentle mockery of the ego, is the one way with modern self-conscious man, to bring him to a humility that is neither the blind alley of an inverted pride nor the precipice of despair.

—Clare Boothe Luce *SNL*, 269

AN ATTACHED HEART

What has prompted me to think, preach, and write about attachment and detachment, about holy indifference, about living with change, was yet another surgery I had eight years after a lung cancer operation. The cancer event had been followed by both radiation and chemotherapy. The radiation damaged the vessels around my heart, so that when the surgeons opened me up for the triple bypass eight years later, they spent the first two hours releasing my heart from all the scar tissue adhesions surrounding it. My heart was literally "attached" to everything and was pulled and pulling in every direction with every beat.

A few years later, when I was scheduled to give a retreat, the retreat coordinator asked me for the retreat's title. The simple word *attached*, drawn from that image of my heart, came to mind and became the retreat title. In the development of that "Attached" retreat, the thoughts for this book emerged.

The retreat itself reflected on our lives as we mature, experience gains and losses, and discover that the terrain of life just keeps changing—whether we want it to or not. I asked retreatants—and now you—what do you hang onto, or try to cling to, and when do you let go? I spoke and now write about being realistic about your human condition and about reflecting on what really matters to you—or at least what you really *want* to matter to you.

As you know, your priorities keep changing throughout life. You hardly care now about some things you were pretty serious about decades ago; such things as grades, going steady, seeing if you could get away with one thing or another under your parents' noses, and so on. With maturity, you discover that some things really don't matter anymore the way they used to, such as winning the football game (or any game for that matter), dancing like a dork, being "the same enough" as everybody else in order to be accepted, and being "different enough" to be oneself.

Is it natural to feel like this? Is there virtue and maturity in these feelings, this way of thinking? Are you just depressed, and don't give a darn? Has your "give-a-darn" just left and abandoned you?

WHO AM I
AND WHO ARE YOU?

Constantly, I try to give my whole life to the Lord—to become more and more aware of God's presence breathing into me love, life, and forgiveness, to bring Jesus to life by the power of the Holy Spirit in everything I do.

This is largely a "my heart to God's heart" approach to living the gospel of Jesus as developed by St. Francis de Sales, the inspiration of the Oblates of St. Francis de Sales, and the religious order, founded by Blessed Father Louis Brisson. As an Oblate priest, I have been schooled in the saint's heart-to-heart approach and discipline to living the gospel in everyday life according to who we are. This spirituality flowing from St. Francis de Sales and his close spiritual friend and correspondent, St. Jane de Chantal, is called "Salesian."[1]

Two brief excerpts from the many works of St. Francis de Sales, a prolific writer and excellent communicator, sum up well his approach to living the gospel according to who you are:

> Let us be who we are and be that well, in order to bring honor to the Master Craftsman whose handiwork we are....Let us be what God wants us to be, provided we are His, and let us not be what we would like to be, contrary to his intention. Even if we were the most perfect creatures under heaven, what good would that do us if we were not as God's will would have us be?"[2]

> I wish, dear lover of God, to engrave and inscribe on your heart, before everything else, this holy and sacred maxim: LIVE JESUS! After that I am sure that your whole life which comes from your heart-center, like the almond tree from its seed, will produce all its actions which are its fruits inscribed and engraved with the same word of salvation. Just as this gentle Jesus will live in your heart, he will live also in your conduct, and appear in your eyes, in your mouth, in your hands, even in your hair. Then you could say reverently following St. Paul: *I live now, not I, but Christ lives in me* (Gal 2:20).[3]

It's not that you always do that so successfully but that it is seriously what you have chosen—and keep on choosing to try to do. There are always many obstacles within yourself and within the world in which you live, obstacles to your doing what you really want to do.

> I do not understand my own actions. For I do not do what I want, but I do the very thing I hate....I can will what is right, but I cannot do it. For I do not do the good I want, but the evil I do not want is what I do. Now if I do what I do not want, it is no longer I that do it, but sin that dwells within me. (Rom 7:15, 18b–20)

You are surrounded by many loves from which to choose. You want to keep things in perspective and always love the Creator whose beauty is glimpsed in created things and is your real home and destination in life.

Because you picked up this book, I assume that you want to do and be the same thing—that is, to keep giving your life to the Lord and to live your whole life for the Lord.

APPROACHING THE SPIRITUAL LIFE

We are on a journey to our heavenly home. Since we can't take anything with us—except, perhaps our character—what should we carry on the journey? What should we care about most? What do we want to hold onto—or have hold onto us? What is a worthwhile attachment?

With everything changing so fast, we have to grasp *something* for stability when we're standing "on the train" and it starts moving and jerking ahead or braking. Of course, on the journey we also need to know when to let go in order to get off the train, either at our destination or to transfer to another train.

In the following twelve chapters, we will explore the experience of living in the world: a world of consumer spending and of accumulating—including nonmaterial things, a world of many values and brain attachments that are different from the gospel of Jesus Christ. Together we will look at how things are attached; our egocentricity; our self-concept; the God concept we hang onto; success, failure, and the need to be right; relationships, jealousies, and the forgiveness of injuries; the gift of sexuality and its problems; prayer and our attachment to God; the need to hang onto the cross of Jesus; living in the present moment; and the ultimate abandonment that is called "holy indifference." To better reflect on what you've read and to integrate it into your daily life, each chapter offers discussion questions and suggested activities.

That incredible Doctor of the Church and Doctor of Divine Love, St. Francis de Sales, has been the foremost influence in my own spiritual journey. So that you can know more about him and his approach to the spiritual life and the spirituality of attachment to God, at the end of the book there are brief biographies of him and St. Jane de Chantal, a brief outline of Salesian spirituality, and some references for further reading. Although Sts. Francis and Jane wrote more than four centuries ago, their thoughts and spiritual counsel still speak to us with wisdom and practicality.

My hope is that you will find their thoughts and approach to the spiritual life as penetrating and inspiring as I do, and that like many who have followed these two wise and holy people, you will learn what to let go of and what to hang onto. With their help, you can cultivate a spirituality of attachment and detachment and develop an attitude and behavior of holy indifference that will simplify your life, reduce anxieties, and lead you to focus on what is essential to Christian living. This is a moderate approach, surely due to the influence of St. Francis de Sales, but as Sr. Anne Marie, VHM, one of his recently deceased Sisters of the Visitation at Georgetown, was fond of saying, "Moderation in all things…including moderation."

NOTES

1. See Appendix III for a brief summary of Salesian spirituality.

2. Letter CCLXXXIX, June 10, 1605, appearing in *LSD*, 111.

3. *IDL*, III, 23.

Chapter 1
Attachment

People are rich in spirit, if their mind is filled with riches or set on riches.

—St. Francis de Sales, *IDL*, III, 14

INSTRUMENTS OF ATTACHMENT

Rubber bands and paperclips are two of God's greatest inventions. They hold things together and can easily be removed. Rubber bands join a huge group of items that help us attach things to other things. Nearly every household boasts a junk drawer filled with tape, nails, twine, and glue.

We are surrounded by instruments of attachment: our bodies use muscle, ligaments, and skin to attach one body part to another. Some of us wear a belt to hold up our pants. Some of us wear a bracelet or necklace made of links chained together. Toddlers pull toys with ropes and handles that allow the toy to move with the child. Our elderly parents wear electronic emergency alerts around their necks. These are examples of how we attach to things in a material way.

How We Attach Things to Other Things	
adhesive tape	paperclip
staple	glue
(continued)	

	(continued)	
duct tape		ball and chain
string		tendons
rope		connective tissue
knots		scar tissue
belt		handcuffs
stitching		contract
bow		covenant
melting together		wedding
welding		coitus
button		umbilical cord
chained		bonding
zipper		affection
pin		need
Velcro		love wrapping
nail		around
screw		gravity
interlocked		prison
loop and hook		rubber band
tether		magnet
leash		Post-it Note

For Francis de Sales, reflecting on our attachments helps us to arrange them—our loves, our addictions—and make decisions about our spiritual lives: what to let go of, or what to minimize, or what to hang onto tighter. If we are going to become wholly indifferent relative to those things that mean less to us, we must get a handle on what we are talking about.

We sometimes speak of being really attached to a dog, cat, or some other pet. Once, when visiting my sisters in Chicago, my sister, Jeanne, who had gotten a new dog since I had last seen her, said to me, "John, you haven't *met* Pepper, have you?" Her use of the word *met* surprised me, and I responded with something silly like, "Well, Pepper Sir, what a pleasure to meet you!" Jeanne had, in short order, become really attached to her dog. Indeed, Pepper was a very fun dog.

We can speak too of being attached to certain people or even practices or places. In church, for example, some people become so attached to a specific pew that they think of it as "my pew." This kind of attachment became quite obvious to me one weekend about an hour before the Saturday afternoon Mass when I was setting up a missions display in an empty church. As I organized my materials on a front row of seats and awaited the arrival of my display table, a man walked over to me, pointed, and said, "I sit right there." He stood and waited for me to move everything so that he could sit on one of a thousand seats that could have been "his."

What do we carry with us along the path of life? What are we attached to both materially *and* spiritually? How good is it, or is it burdensome?

The method to attach things varies, of course, according to the materials being attached. We wisely use each attachment method or instrument according to the requirements of the materials and the usefulness of the particular method. For example, we don't use a welding torch to attach two pieces of paper, nor do we use tape to attach steel panels when building a ship. Having a wide variety of possibilities for attachment is practical and makes life easier!

Other considerations when attaching two items are the permanence and flexibility of the desired attachment. For example, it is very useful to be able to zip up a jacket in a cold wind, attaching the jacket's front two sides to each other, but it is also valuable to be able to unzip the jacket once inside. The paper clip that holds papers together also allows us to rearrange pages and then hold them together again in a different order.

To be able to attach and detach some things is important, while in other cases we really want the attachment to last forever, or at least for a long time. We intend permanence when we glue down linoleum in the kitchen, screw in a door's hinge, or stitch closed an open wound so that it can more easily heal. Yet many attachments are very useful as long as they can be detached—if and when we want them to be.

RUNNING WITH SUITCASES

Having too many things attached to us starts to get bulky or heavy, and makes even walking around the block more difficult, let alone trying to run a race. Picture yourself in a marathon, running with suitcases, grocery bags, and a ball and chain attached to each leg. In order to reach the finish line, it surely helps to be as unburdened—as unattached—as possible.

A spiritual life with too many attachments cannot only be difficult but perhaps even impossible, particularly when we have attachments to the sins in our lives. In *Introduction of the Devout Life*, written for everyday people desiring to live a holy life devoted to the Lord, St. Francis de Sales talks not only about severing ourselves from our *attachments* to serious sin but distancing ourselves from our *affections* for sin.

> All the Israelites did in fact leave the land of Egypt where they were enslaved, but they did not all leave it in so far as attachment to it was concerned. That is why, in the desert, many of them were sad that they did not have the onions and meat of Egypt (Num 11:4–5). In the same way there are penitents who in fact leave sin but do not leave their attachment to it. In other words they intend not to sin again but they give up and deny themselves the pleasures of sin with a certain

reluctance. Though their heart turns away from sin and leaves it behind, yet it does not stop looking back again and again in that direction as Lot's wife did towards Sodom (Gen 19:26)....They would like very much if they could sin and not be damned.[1]

It is as if we the Israelites are moaning, "If only murder weren't a sin, or cookies didn't have calories, or the pleasure of sex didn't have consequences in relationship. Boy, what I would do then!" Or boasting, "If only revenge weren't forbidden by Jesus, you wouldn't want to see what I'd do to him! Lucky for him, but too bad for me." However, Francis de Sales continues,

As you desire to commit yourself to the devout life, you must not only turn away from sin, but you must completely cut away from your heart every attachment connected with sin. Otherwise, there is first of all the danger of falling back into sin. Besides these unhappy attachments will constantly weaken your spirit, and make it sluggish, so that you will not be able to do good works promptly, carefully, and frequently, for it is in this that the true essence of being devoted consists.[2]

ARE SOME ATTACHMENTS NECESSARY?

Realistically, either some things (material and spiritual) will always cling to us and not let go, or we will choose to hang onto them. We aren't spiritual angels without bodies. We are flesh-and-blood human beings, thoroughly human, and still a work in progress. So we don't even want to try to be good angels, since that isn't what we are or what God created us to be. We want to be good women and men, good people, who we are as best we can. Being who we are and who we have been made to be will give glory to God, whose masterpieces we are. As St. Irenaeus (AD 125–202) once said, "The glory of God is the human person fully alive."[3]

Only a few of us are willing or able to streak down the track, like Isaiah the prophet did.

> [A]t that time the LORD had spoken to Isaiah son of Amoz, saying "Go, and loose the sackcloth from your loins and take your sandals off your feet," and he had done so, walking naked and barefoot. Then the LORD said, "Just as my servant Isaiah has walked naked and barefoot for three years as a sign and a portent against Egypt and Ethiopia, so shall the king of Assyria lead away the Egyptians as captives and the Ethiopians as exiles, both the young and the old, naked and barefoot, with buttocks uncovered, to the shame of Egypt." (Isa 20:2–4)

St. Francis of Assisi is said to have made such a gesture as well. When his father took him to the bishop's court to get back the money Francis had begun spending on repairing San Damiano Church, Francis repaid him, "renounced his inheritance, and took off his clothes and gave them back as well. A laborer's smock was found for him to wear, and this public renunciation of his inheritance and of the world marked his conversion to a life of poverty and dedication of himself to God."[4]

However, even if we were to get detached from everything and walk (or streak) the journey in our birthday suits, it would hardly be a permanent condition but perhaps more a freedom lark done on a dare. Realistically, we need to get comfortable carrying around and being attached to *some* things and to make choices about what we want to stay attached to, how strong we want the attachments to be, and how permanent or temporary we can make the attachments.

We can't be totally detached from everything, or at least for long—not many of us, if any, can do that. We know that we never have to be—or can be—angels or pure spirits on this earth. Rather, we *can* strive to be good, human, earthbound men and women with not only a spiritual life, but a material one as well.

In the next chapter, we will look at our attachments and ask how necessary or important they are. Are we able to still be joyful even if we lose everything there is to lose?

SCRIPTURE REFLECTION

Therefore, since we are surrounded by so great a cloud of witnesses, let us also lay aside every weight and the sin that clings so closely, and let us run with perseverance the race that is set before us, looking to Jesus the pioneer and perfecter of our faith (Heb 12:1–2).

QUESTIONS FOR REFLECTION

1. When has an attachment hindered my freedom? Increased my freedom?

2. Is it fair to speak of things as attachments, or are they just a part of who I am?

3. What values or considerations should determine how long I hang onto something, whether spiritual or material? Do I hang onto it out of habit, usefulness, potential, tradition, revenge, sadness?

SUGGESTED ACTIVITY

In order to discern what you are attached to, take a sheet of paper, and at the top, label five columns: I'm Attached, Attached How, Positive, Negative, Interesting. In the first "I'm Attached" column, list a few of your material and spiritual/emotional attachments. In the next column, identify how that attachment clings to you. Across the next three columns, identify why the attachment is a positive or negative for you. Some attachments may simply be "Interesting"—not positive or negative.

I'm Attached	Attached How	Positive	Negative	Interesting
to my car	by need and like	I've got wheels	It is costly	
to my opinion	like my skin	I have conviction	I seem to be a know-it-all	

NOTES

1. *IDL*, I, 7; MSFS Translation, 48.

2. Ibid., 49.

3. This is an excerpt from his monumental work written about AD 185, *Against Heresies* (Lib. 4, 20, 5–7; SC 100, 640–42, 644–48) which was in large part responsible for exposing the absurdities of Gnosticism and laying out the first somewhat systematic exposition of the apostolic and Catholic faith. This reading is used in the Roman Office of Readings on the feast (liturgical memorial) of Saint Irenaeus on June 28.

4. *Butlers Lives of the Saints: October*, New Full Edition (Collegeville, MN: The Liturgical Press, 1997), 18.

Chapter 2

Possessions

Poverty of spirit is a detachment from all created things, if we possess them. This poverty of spirit requires us not to set our affection on these, so that we must be poor in these things in affection and will, by having our heart detached and wholly free, being equally contented to have them not or to have them.

—St. Jane de Chantal, *CJC*, 235

CLINGING TO POSSESSIONS

As modern materialists, we are already the world's lottery winners; we are very dependent on many things and frequently whine that we want more. Perhaps we have often thought that we want more money, but rarely does anybody *really* want the money. Money, itself, is fairly useless unless you give it away to a merchant for a purchase, to a friend as a gift, or to a cause to accomplish some good. Otherwise, money just sits and either grows or declines in value without really doing anything. How interested would you be if, in a cloud of smoke, a genie came out of a lamp and offered you a billion dollars under the following conditions: you can't tell anybody you have the money, you can't spend the money or any return on its investment, and you can't give it away or will it to others? If you break any of these conditions, the money will disappear as quickly as it appeared. Would you still want the money? I doubt it, but perhaps only to see if you could cheat fate. The reason we want money is to be able to give it away!

Like most people, I know about letting go of money because I have no problem spending it! However, when it comes to possessions, like many, I am not so adept at letting go. For example, I still possess a box of college notes taken during the Cenozoic Era and a handful of photos from the time in first grade when I served as a page boy for the bishop.

Some of us accumulate books like iron filings cling to a magnet. Why do we own so many books? It's not that we don't read them, or at least really *want* to read them. We like learning, but in gathering more books than we can possibly read, are we trying to convince ourselves that we're intellectual? Are we trying to prove something to ourselves? Are we trying to impress somebody? I haven't figured that out for myself; have you?

We may never truly know the conscious or unconscious motivations or emotions that lead us to keep lots of possessions. We all exist somewhere on a long, drawn-out continuum of *hoarders*. Each of us probably knows an extreme hoarder (or you've seen one on TV): someone who can never throw away anything and whose house is no more than a pathway between stacked stuff— old newspapers, magazines, and defunct appliances stacked in huge piles to the ceiling. Most of us aren't that extreme in our own acts of hanging onto things; nor are many of us starkly monastic and simple.

A few years ago while in Austin, Texas, to preach a parish mission, I stayed with a family: a mom, dad, and two children. In their home all the walls and ceilings were white, the furniture was elegant, simple wood, and the windows were attractive with no shades or curtains. There was no clutter and all the decorations were sparse yet attractive. I was amazed that people actually lived there—much less two kids! The family had lived there for several years and clearly earned enough money to decorate the home as fully as they wanted. Astonished by the cleanliness and beautiful simplicity of the home and all its appointments, I felt like my presence somehow cluttered the place. This was the other end of that continuum.

GETTING RID OF POSSESSIONS

Modern life makes accumulating stuff easier than ever, with TV shopping channels, one-click online shopping options, and the proliferation of Web sites that promote buying, making, and wanting more stuff in order to be considered cool and in sync with what millions of others own.

Curiously, and rather sadly, not only have we become a culture that collects or hoards things, but we have, by our actions, created a burgeoning industry of books, programs, plans, and paid consultants that help us *get rid of things*. Resources abound about how to reduce clutter and organize our closets, garages, basements, and anything that can store our belongings.

It's amazing every January to see the racks of magazines featuring articles about how to declutter and organize our homes and workplaces. The process often starts by cleaning out any clothes or shoes we haven't worn for x number of months or years, and then determining whether this stuff is worthy of giving away to the St. Vincent de Paul Society, Goodwill, or the Salvation Army, or pitching it altogether. We wonder whether someone else can wear this item. Is this cloth worthy only of becoming rags or is it a total pitch? Just exercising such choices indicates the affluence of our culture and how well we are doing, even someone like me who took a vow of poverty and lives in a religious community.

Amid all our stuff, we may ask ourselves if we have embarrassingly too much while other people have almost nothing. What should we keep because we really use it and need it, and what can we give away?

Trees uprooted by the wind are not fit for transplanting because their roots are left behind in the soil; but if they are to be moved to another plot of ground their roots must be deftly and gradually disengaged one by one. And because we are to be transplanted from this miserable earth to the land of the living we must loosen our affections one by one from this world. I am not saying that we should roughly sever all the ties we have formed but we must disentangle ourselves from them and loosen their hold upon us. (St. Francis de Sales, *LST*, 54–55)

At one time, I visited the ministry of Mother Teresa of Calcutta's Sisters in the city of Bangalore, India. The Sisters housed and cared for two hundred people unable to care for themselves. One young man, who looked to be in his early twenties, was scooting around on his tail end, with a piece of cardboard under his butt for protection. His legs obviously didn't work at all. One Sister said to me, "Father, Joseph loves to sing." And then she looked at Joseph and said, "Sing for Father, Joseph." The young man took my hand and started swinging it (a gesture that I had seen men do in India, and culturally, it certainly doesn't mean what you might think it means in the United States). At the same time, he began singing, "God is so good, God is so good, God is so good, he's so good to me." I looked to the heavens and addressed God, "What's the deal, Lord? He is happier than I am. If I had brain damage from birth that permanently paralyzed my legs, and my family who could no longer manage to take care of me left me in a mission, and then some Sister asked me to sing, you know what I would sing, don't you? 'Nobody knows the trouble I've seen; nobody knows but Jesus.'"

I felt embarrassed because Joseph seemed to be so much more grateful than I was, and yet he barely had a pot to piddle in. I have had so much—from a super education to great medical care, from a closet full of clothes to the current technologies of doing business. As a person in the affluent culture of the United States, I had taken a lot for granted, and I had a very long way to go toward becoming more grateful. I was one of those nine of ten lepers healed by Jesus who didn't return to say thank you (Luke 17:11–19).

BEING MORE GRATEFUL

The first part of a spirituality of hanging onto and letting go of material things is to focus on being more grateful. That takes regular practice. I learned this whenever I joined Kevin and Claudia and their five children for dinner. I was struck how, before saying the grace before a meal, each person around the table mentioned something he or she was grateful for that day.

Gratitude is something we can practice for a lifetime. It is a lifestyle we adopt. It is a truism that grateful people are happy people. We can practice being grateful in many ways, such as sponsoring a poor child and writing to the child every month; checking in regularly on an aging person who may not have anyone doing so; daily putting a dollar in a jar for someone who needs the money more than us; or listing every night in a journal three things we are grateful for this day. Each of these actions requires regular practice.

Have you thought much—or at all—about what you want to do to practice gratefulness? If you haven't given much thought to doing this, here are simple ways to begin:

- Stock a drawer in your favorite desk with postage stamps, thank-you cards and a selection of other cards, and your addresses. (You may want to do this near your computer or smartphone that holds contacts.) Resist the easy temptation of sending an e-mail, text, or Facebook message, and instead adopt a habit of handwriting a personal note that says you took time and effort to express your gratitude. Be creative and fun with your notes and spontaneous in sending them.

- Put a dollar bill in your pocket or purse every morning and see if you can give it away every day simply because you can. If you think you can do more, make it two or five dollars. Or if you can only do less, make it a quarter or two. (You could even do this with a chunk of your time rather than money.) If you've been blessed a lot, one way of showing gratitude for those gifts is sharing them with someone else—especially for no particular reason. Be a model of God's grace that is freely given, undeserved, not earned, just spontaneous, even impulsive, yet deliberately generous expressing thanks to life, thanks to God, for all that is.

- Once in a while or once a week, fast from your normal diet by cutting in half or by two-thirds the size of your meals, or even more if your health permits. Stand in solidarity with those brothers and sisters who have much less to eat today.

- Travel for a weekend, a week, or longer with a mission-based group that serves the poor here or abroad to learn how other people live with less stuff. My own perspective on global poverty has been radically affected by my travels and seeing how little most of the world lives on and how much we have, I have. That change in perspective itself has been a great motivation for trying to simplify my lifestyle, not in a radical way of living on almost nothing but by not wanting to be such an incredible over-consumer, especially of things I don't really need. Ask yourself, "What possessions are really important for me

to hang onto, helping me be truly myself and truly free?"
Let go of what would make it easier for you to have more
freedom.

No one is ever ready to admit that he or she is avari-
cious (having too great a desire for wealth). Everyone
denies having so base and mean a heart. One man
excuses himself on the score that he has to take care of
his children...and that prudence requires that he be a
man of property. He never has too much; he always
finds need for more....Avarice is a raging fever that
makes itself all the harder to detect the more violent
and burning it is. If you are strongly attached to the
goods you possess, are too solicitous about them, set
your heart on them, always have them in your
thoughts, and fear losing them with a strong, anxious
fear, then, believe me, you are still subject to such fever.
(St. Francis de Sales, *IDL* III, 14)

SCRIPTURE REFLECTION

A certain ruler asked him, "Good Teacher, what must I
do to inherit eternal life?" Jesus said to him, "Why do
you call me good? No one is good but God alone. You
know the commandments: 'You shall not commit adultery; You shall not murder; You shall not steal; You
shall not bear false witness; Honor your father and
mother.'" He replied, "I have kept all these since my
youth." When Jesus heard this, he said to him, "There
is still one thing lacking. Sell all that you own and dis-
tribute the money to the poor, and you will have treasure in heaven; then come, follow me." But when he
heard this, he became sad; for he was very rich. Jesus

looked at him and said, "How hard it is for those who have wealth to enter the kingdom of God! Indeed, it is easier for a camel to go through the eye of a needle than for someone who is rich to enter the kingdom of God." Those who heard it said, "Then who can be saved?" He replied, "What is impossible for mortals is possible for God." Then Peter said, "Look, we have left our homes and followed you." And he said to them, "Truly I tell you, there is no one who has left house or wife or brothers or parents or children, for the sake of the kingdom of God who will not get back very much more in this age, and in the age to come eternal life." (Luke 18:18–30).

QUESTIONS FOR REFLECTION

1. Is this chapter relevant to me? In what ways do I agree or disagree with it?

2. How much of what I have do I want to let go of or give away?

3. What do possessions have to do with spirituality anyhow?

SUGGESTED ACTIVITIES

1. Strategize and plan some gratitude exercises inspired by thoughts in this chapter and your own creativity.

2. Make a plan for regularly giving away things and simplifying your life. Review the plan quarterly or annually to see what you've done and how you might improve your behaviors.

3. Travel to the part of a country where missionaries work among some of the poorest people in the world. If you cannot travel, search for and watch a documentary or attend a lecture about a part of the world that is impoverished.

Chapter 3
It's All about Me!

It is not possible to empty ourselves completely of ourselves. While we are here below, and until such time that God bears us up to heaven, we must always bear with ourselves....Please be patient with everyone, but, first of all, with yourself.

—St. Francis de Sales to Madame Brulart,
March 1605, *LSD*, 108

EGOCENTRICITY

Most of us are egocentric—centered on ourselves—attached to self-centeredness, or perhaps we should call it self-centered self-love.

Evolution's long process has equipped us with a self-centeredness that may have been necessary for our survival in a precivilized world. Eons ago, those hominids, who were more self-centered and primarily self-serving, tended to live longer than others in a primitive and violent world, and thereby lived to reproduce and pass on their genes of self-priority.

Consequently, egocentricity comes quite naturally to us. Even though it may have not only outlived its usefulness today, its dominance has actually become counterproductive in the kingdom of God that Jesus envisions. Jesus calls us to a quantum leap beyond where we are—loving us where we are but calling us to so much more. To love one another, we have to go beyond our nearly exclusive attachment to egocentricity.

When I preach at parish missions about egocentricity, I stand front and center and twirl around a few times while singing:

It's all about me, it's all about me,
it's **not** about you, it's all about **me**,
why can't you see?[1]

Deep inside, I know that's what I keep rediscovering about myself. Everyone in the congregation laughs because they know I am making fun of all of us.

Of course, there's the joke: "How many teenagers does it take to unscrew a light bulb?" The answer: "Just one who hangs onto the bulb and waits for the universe to rotate around him or her." I twirl again in front. The people laugh harder, but that's unfair to teenagers only because it's true for the rest of us as well.

HIDDEN EGOCENTRICITY

Years ago, I did not think of myself as self-centered. Instead, I usually thought of myself according to the ideals that I projected for myself in life, that is, how I *wanted* to be, and that clearly included an other-centeredness that is necessary if one is going to be a "lover" like Jesus. I never realized how deeply hidden my egocentricity was—especially from me.

Before being ordained for ministry, I took a Clinical Pastoral Education course at St. Michael's Hospital in Toronto, Canada, where I served on the chaplains' team and visited patients with the goal of learning how to better "minister" to others in the hospital. One day, I was given the name of a terminal patient to visit. Before entering that patient's room, I learned that he was sixty-two years old, with terminal cancer and only months to live. When I went to the man's bedside, he saw my badge from the pastoral care department and that I was a chaplain, and he began swearing at me, cursing God, and chasing me from his room.

In my meeting with my supervisor, I said, "Father Al, you are going to have to assign me another patient." When he asked why, I explained what had happened. He then asked me, "John, whose needs did you respond to today?" I said, "Pardon me?" He clarified for me and said, "The man is dying with cancer. You knew that before you got there. You promptly learned how angry the man is, seemingly specifically at God. So you left. And now you want another patient. Should I give you instead someone who will appreciate you more as a chaplain? Who is this really about, anyway? It seems like you took care of *your* needs to escape from someone who wasn't appreciating you, but you did nothing at all for him who is dying. Perhaps you should reassess whether you are really interested in serving others."

I was embarrassed and frustrated, and blurted out, "What was I *supposed* to do?" Father Al simply said, "How about coming to me and asking how you can help the guy, instead of just writing him off and asking for another patient who *would* appreciate you." So we role-played the scenario and worked out some responses for such a situation like the following: "It sounds like you're pretty angry. Can you tell me about that?"

In trying to help someone, I discovered that "it's still all about me!" I have never forgotten that lesson, although I continue learning how much of my thinking and behavior is primarily about me, and keep gently taking the tiniest evolutionary step toward other-centered love. And then I am so pleased with myself, as if the universe noticed!

Self-centered love is like a *default* on a computer—a method of operating—unless we've selected something else to override it. It comes as naturally to us as breathing. It is as much a part of us as if it is a genetic attachment. Furthermore, unless we are consciously aware and deliberately choose to act beyond that self-centeredness, what we get is, "It's all about me."

BALANCING NEEDS

Self-centered love is absolutely necessary, not only for survival, but even if we are going to move beyond it. Unless we take care of ourselves and our own needs, we might never be in good enough condition to care for another's needs.

Reviewing my patient visit at St. Michael's hospital, I could see I felt a need to be appreciated. I didn't realize it, and my self-centered "ego-terrorist" sabotaged my ability to help the patient. Once I could recognize *my* need for appreciation, I could either take care of that need in order to pay attention to the patient's need, or I could consciously put my need on hold until later.

When I returned to see my dying friend again, he laughed when I walked in the room and said, "I didn't think you'd come back after the way I hollered at you the other day." Thereafter, I was able to companion him in his last weeks.

Parents learn by necessity to balance their own need with the needs of their children. The parents might need a good night's sleep before going to work the next day, but they will take a temporary pass on that need when there is a very sick child during the night. Balancing your own needs and the needs of children can be a major exercise in dying to dominant self-centered love.

An incident that happened while I was traveling illustrates the importance of recognizing and balancing needs. Once, upon checking out of a hotel, I observed a hotel desk clerk who checked out the gentleman ahead of me and asked the man how his night was. The man said, "It was terrible. Every fifteen minutes there was banging on the wall that woke me up." The clerk apologized and said that he hoped the man's next stay at this hotel would be a better experience. Just after the man left, a young couple came to check out, and the clerk asked them too how their night was. "It was terrible," they said. "The man in the room next to us snored so loudly that we couldn't get to sleep, so we kept pounding on the wall to wake him so that we might fall asleep."

Balancing needs is sometimes a tricky proposition. As human beings, we are a developing species, and it's clear that we are not angels, nor are we likely ever to be angels. Therefore, any expectations of consistent angelic behavior from me or anybody else are simply delusional.

Who we are is thoroughly *hum*an.
Pretty *hum*orous in our self-delusions.
*Hum*ble in reality but puffed up in pretense.
Made of the same stuff as *hum*us.

In a letter to Mademoiselle de Soulfour, dated July 22, 1603, the Bishop of Geneve (Francis de Sales) advised the young woman on a number of topics, but principally on acceptance of herself as a human being and being realistic about her spiritual progress based on that condition.

Know that patience is the one virtue which gives greatest assurance of our reaching perfection, and while we must have patience with others, we must also have it with ourselves. Those who aspire to the pure love of God need to be more patient with themselves than with others. We have to endure our own imperfections in order to attain perfection....In truth we have to admit that we are weak creatures who scarcely do anything well; but God, who is infinitely kind, is satisfied with our small achievement and is very pleased with the preparation of our heart....I have one thing to tell you, so remember it well, we are sometimes so busy being good angels that we neglect to be good men and women.[2]

Being detached completely from self-centered love simply doesn't work. After all, Jesus never said we shouldn't love ourselves at all, but rather asks us to use our self-love as the comparison for how we should love others: "You shall *love* the Lord your God with all your heart, and with all your soul, and with all your strength, and with all your mind; and *your neighbor as yourself*" (Luke 10:27, emphasis by author).

> Consequently, we are left with the challenge of being conscious of our humanness and our natural tendency toward self-centeredness, and with the assistance of God's grace, to practice on a daily basis being centered on someone outside of ourselves, which does not come naturally to us most of the time. One of the best exercises of meekness we can perform is never to fret at our own imperfections. Although reason requires that we should be displeased and sorry when we commit any fault, yet we must refrain from a bitter, gloomy, spiteful, and passionate displeasure. In this many are greatly to blame who, on being overcome by anger, are angry for having been angry, troubled at being troubled, and vexed at being vexed. By this means they keep their heart drenched and steeped in passion. Although it seems as if the second anger destroys the first, it serves nevertheless to open a passage for fresh anger on the first occasion that presents itself.
>
> Believe me, just as the mild and affectionate reproofs of a father have far greater power to correct his child than rage and passion, so when we have committed any fault, if we reprehend our heart with mild and calm remonstrances, having more compassion for it than passion against it, and encourage it to amendment, the repentance it shall conceive by this means will sink much deeper, and penetrate it more effectually, than a

fretful, angry, and stormy repentance. (St. Francis de Sales, *IDL*, 3:9)

BEING OTHER-CENTERED

Prayer and meditation can help greatly with the conscious reflection on the motives behind our thought and behaviors. That's one of the main ways we can increasingly become more aware of our own self-centeredness. It is also critical to meditate on the life and situation of others—from the Jesus of the Gospels, to the people in the daily news, to the people with whom we live or daily associate—"walking a mile in their moccasins." This is all part of the process of awareness of the world beyond ourselves.

A person cannot be much of a lover if he or she cannot control that ego-terrorist. And to say "that's just the way I am" is ridiculously limiting in ways that most people won't accept in our lives. We can and do learn many things that don't come naturally to us, like training our fingers to play a piano or navigate a computer keyboard. In a similar way, we develop many other skills we want in our lives: singing, golfing, guitar playing, dancing, pole vaulting, cooking, and so on. We all know the old joke, "How do you get to Carnegie Hall?" "Practice! Practice! Practice!"

Specific resolutions that focus our attention, love, and care on the others in our lives can produce some behavioral little steps of balance and improvement in our transformation into the loving Christ. However, it requires a daily consciousness and discipline to make this a regular habit, which is what real lovers do—habitually try to find ways to express love to others. For Christians, that includes everyone—even our enemies.

Continually discovering the roots of self-centered behavior shouldn't be a surprise. New shoots spring up all the time, even if it seems that we've cut them back to the ground. We can change the self-centeredness within us, but it never really dies. We need to balance it every day with our attempts at other-centeredness.

We need to be patient. Each of us is a work in progress. In reality, we know that we are foolish and delusional to think that we can, or already have, totally detached ourselves from self-centered love. It's not even a goal, quite honestly. Our self-centeredness is one of those attachments that perhaps we can reduce to a button and buttonhole, that can be attached or not at will, rather than something welded in the genes of our evolutionary past over which we have no control.

> It is not possible to empty ourselves completely of ourselves. While we are here below, and until such time that God bears us up to heaven, we must always bear with ourselves....So we must be patient and not think we can overcome in a day all the bad habits we have acquired through the poor care we have taken of our spiritual health.
>
> God did cure some people instantly, without leaving within them a trace of their former illness, as in the case of Mary Magdalen....On the other hand, this same God left in several of his dear disciples many marks of their evil inclinations for some time after their conversion, all for their greater good: for example, blessed St. Peter who stumbled many times after his initial calling and who one occasion failed totally and miserably by denying the Lord (Matt 26:69–75)....
>
> [Besides] there is a great danger that the soul which has catered to its own passions and affections over a long period of time might become proud and vain if in a moment it could master them completely. We must, little by little and step by step, acquire that self-mastery which the saints took years to acquire. Please be patient with everyone, but, first of all, with

yourself." (St. Francis de Sales to Madame Brulart, March 1605, *LSD*, 108)

SCRIPTURE REFLECTION

So if I, your Lord and Teacher, have washed your feet, you also ought to wash one another's feet. For I have set you an example, that you also should do as I have done to you (John 13:14–15).

QUESTIONS FOR REFLECTION

1. In what ways do I recognize myself as self-centered, or do I only see others as self-centered?

2. What daily strategies can I design for myself to grow in other-centeredness?

3. Do I have effective prayer rituals for holding my goals before me on a daily basis?

SUGGESTED ACTIVITIES

1. Imagine "being" another person, perhaps, for example, Jesus' mother Mary at the foot of the cross, or a father holding his child after a violent incident, or an elderly infirm patient whose memory is seriously failing.

2. Take a trip to some very poor part of the country or the world and become more aware of the lives that people lead there.

3. Look to the events and people of the day ahead as you dress in the morning and plan how you might pay more attention to their needs in the simplest of ways,

asking the Lord to help you put on kindness, compassion, patience, and a smile.

NOTES

1. This is sung to the melody of "It Had To Be You," by Isham Jones with lyrics by Gustav Kahn, 1924.

2. Nancy Jayne Bowden, "'Ma Très Chère Fille': The Spirituality of François de Sales and Jeanne de Chantal and the Enablement of Women," (PhD thesis, University of Washington, 1995). This study is an exploration of the enabling qualities and effects of Salesian spirituality on the lives of women.

Chapter 4

Who Do I Think I Am?

Some people become proud and insolent because they ride a fine horse, wear a feather in their hat, or are dressed in a fine suit of clothes. Who does not see the folly of this? For if there is any value in such things, doesn't the glory really belong to the horse, the bird, and the tailor. What meanness of heart it is to borrow esteem from a horse, a feather, or from some passing fashion!

—St. Francis de Sales, *IDL,* 3:4

WORD MADE FLESH

When I was a young priest, I met a nineteen-year-old in the neighborhood where I was working. Rex was a tough, streetwise young man with a rough attitude toward life. One hot summer day, I stopped by his house to say hello, and he met me on the front sidewalk. I asked him how he was, and he answered that he was going on a trip. "Where?" I asked. He told me that he was going to kill himself.

"O Lord, help! Help him! Help me right now to know what to do and say," I prayed silently. I got Rex to sit with me in the car. I was committed to staying with him, since he couldn't very well kill himself while I was there, and I had no sense that I was in any danger. We drove to my place where we could sit and talk, and I could spend whatever time with him I could. No matter how much I searched for evidence to use against his desire to commit suicide, he kept circling back to one persistent theme: "I ain't worth shit." He hadn't achieved much in life that I could remind him of so as to encourage him.

Since we seemed to be spinning our wheels and getting nowhere, I started praying again to know what to do. The mental image I kept seeing was one arm held out to Rex and the other reaching straight up to God begging for help. That's my "capital L" prayer—one arm reaching out, the other reaching heavenward while crying out, "Help!"

My experience is that often God speaks very few words, but clear ones. The words this time seemed to say, "Hug him." I thought, "O God, no! This is Rex. He'll punch me. This must not be your idea, God, but my half-Lebanese background that believes a hug will fix anything." So I went back to the capital L prayer. I got the same answer. I tried again, but only got that one answer, "Hug him." I don't think I was convinced of the authenticity of the inspiration, but I didn't have any other ideas.

Standing up in front of Rex, I said, "Stand up, I want to do something." He answered, "What?" with a tone that scared me a bit as he stood up. I said, "I want to give you a hug." I opened my arms, and he grabbed me in a bear hug that I thought might break some ribs. He held me, and held me, and held me, and then he started crying, sobbing, and blubbering. My prayer was, "Thank you, Lord; sorry I took so long to follow through on your directions." Words weren't making any difference to Rex, but word made flesh? That was another story.

SELF-WORTH

Many of us struggle with self-worth issues, both negative and positive. The problem is in truly knowing ourselves, our dignity, our gifts, our limitations, and our character defects. Our estimations of ourselves are frequently unreal, sometimes even delusional, and we can be very attached to that delusional image, like lint on wool that just won't easily be brushed away.

Like Rex, many of us have suffered from a negativity because of what has happened in our lives, what others have done to us, and the poor decisions we ourselves have made. Religious fixation on sin, guilt, and sometimes shame can end up depressing us further and blinding us to our inherent worth. Of course, we may often think, "It's all about me. I'm too fat. I'm too dumb. I'm not popular enough. I, I, I, me, me, me."

With such a weak sense of our inherent value, we sometimes try borrowing our value, our self-worth, from such superficial things as our good looks, clothes, cars, bank accounts, popularity, or successes in life, relationships, and business. However, none of these things is truly us; they are just borrowed, and in our hearts we know that they don't seriously speak to our deep-down value.

So, what is our inherent value or essence? It's not the very stuff that we're made of, at least materially. Our body mass is largely carbon, nitrogen, hydrogen, oxygen, and so on, and basically the same list of chemicals on the periodic chart that make up everything else in the universe. Even then, there aren't much of the expensive elements—like gold or silver, for instance. If there were, an obesity epidemic might at least be enriching—worth our weight in gold! Rather, if we could be reduced to the chemicals of our physical composition, we'd each be worth only a buck or two, if that.

Work, health, and wealth are frequently the foci of our attention and effort, and are often counted as our worth. However, these are temporary and can sometimes disappear without leaving a forwarding address: one head-on collision, one crime, one clot; one diagnosis, one national disaster, one depression; one fire, one fatal decision, one failure in business…and all that work, health, and wealth might be lost forever. Good stuff, but not to be counted on particularly.

TOUCHED BY GOD

As believers in God, we can start estimating our worth by looking at the master craftsman who made us. A painting is valuable today because of its painter, not the paint itself or the canvas; it's what the *painter* did with the paint and canvas. Similarly, a sculpture is valuable because of what the sculptor did with the materials and who the sculptor is. When the artist is famous and considered a world-class artist, anything he or she did or does becomes more valuable: a violin made by Stradivarius; a statue chiseled by Michelangelo; a painting by Georgia O'Keeffe or Picasso; music by Hildegard of Bingen or George Gershwin; or a performance by Meryl Streep, Dustin Hoffman, or Aretha Franklin.

We are valuable because of our *Creator*—the mighty God and Creator of everything. I am made by God, touched by God, desired and willed by God into being. God is the master craftsman. I am one of God's masterpieces. So the best thing I can be is me, as God made me and hoped for me to be—my best self.

Furthermore, I am beautiful in God's eyes. I am the apple of God's eye. "You are precious in my sight, and honored, and I love you" (Isa 43:4). The Lord cared for his people, "guarded [them] as the apple of his eye" (Deut 32:10).

I belong to God who loves me, and it's not about me and how good I have to be before I am loved, it's about God: "You are a people holy to the LORD your God; the LORD your God has chosen you out of all the peoples on earth to be his people, his treasured possession. It was not because you were more numerous than any other people that the LORD set his heart on you and chose you— for you were the fewest of all peoples. It was because the LORD loved you" (Deut 7:6–8).

Furthermore, it is God in Jesus Christ who has given his life for me: "The Lord Jesus Christ...gave himself for our sins to set us free from the present evil age, according to the will of our God and Father" (Gal 1:3–4). We must be worth a great deal for God to do that, don't you think? In fact, we are considered a temple of God's presence: "Do you not know that you are God's temple and that God's Spirit dwells in you?" (1 Cor 3:16). Many churches have tabernacles for housing the eucharistic bread of God's presence, and there are tabernacles in the pews as well when the people are gathered.

St. Paul identifies us as the very body of Christ: "Now you are the body of Christ and individually members of it" (1 Cor 12:27). Again, on the walls in many churches there are Stations of the Cross highlighting moments in the passion and death of Jesus, and there are also the stations of our crosses represented by each of us in the pews: the body of Christ, condemned, falling, carrying the cross, and being stripped and nailed.

WE ARE HOLY

It is because *God* has made us, *God* lives in us, and *God* has loved us enough to save us that we can be called "holy." The Bible says that *God* is the holy one, and then applies the word *holy* to us, his people, over eighty times. *We* are only holy because *God* is holy, not because our behavior makes us holy. It's not about me; it's about God. If we really knew our holiness, our dignity, and the holiness and dignity of all creation and every person, we would most naturally treat ourselves and everyone else quite differently, and with higher regard and better care. Compare, for example, a person's treatment of a throwaway paper plate and an expensive heirloom piece of grandmother's china. One is thrown away, while the other is especially cared for because we know its value and meaning to us. Similarly, compare how we might treat a twenty-year-old rusted Plymouth or a banged up VW van to a new luxury Cadillac or Mercedes. How careful (full of care) are we with the latter compared to the former?

Indeed, if we can see ourselves and others as holy and beloved, precious in God's eyes, and belonging to God, we will try to behave according to who we are, and restrict behaviors that would be damaging to our dignity or that of others. In other words, we would want to grow to be more who we really are— beloved temples of God's sacred presence; in essence, we would want to grow in holiness.

Sin is not part of who we really are or who God created us to be. And yet, it is our current human condition, and we have all suffered from it and caused others to suffer as well, sometimes a lot. However, sin isn't really a part of us. Unfortunately, it sticks to us like glue, and every time we detach from it, soon enough we find it reattached. It's sticky, icky, and smelly too. Often, we get deluded by thinking that we are sin itself—not lovable, faulty, self-centered, not worthy, and so on. We whine that nobody loves me and can get really attached to this idea, even finding it unavoidably attractive.

So ask yourself the following: What self-image do I hold onto? Is it revisable? What help do I need to see myself more like God sees me?

BEING FOUND

Of course, it is also possible to see ourselves in an unrealistically positive way; not so much on God's terms but on our own. When workers at a one company were asked to rank themselves (anonymously) as below average, average, or above average compared to the rest of the workforce, an unbelievably large majority of workers rated themselves (impossibly) as above average. Some of us frequently and regularly judge ourselves to be better than others, though the evidence is scant and prejudicial, to say the least.

The parable of the Pharisee and publican (Luke 18:9–14) shines light on this human tendency to think of ourselves as better than others. While the Pharisee thanked God that he was not like others, the tax collector, a despised man in the community, asked God to be merciful to him, a sinner. Jesus told the crowd, "All who exalt themselves will be humbled, but all who humble themselves will be exalted."

We see now "who I am" in dignity (the image of God, the body of Christ, a temple of the Holy Spirit) and how off the mark our attitudes and behaviors sometimes are. We are like the legendary Holy Grail (the cup Jesus used at the Last Supper)—immensely valuable because of who has touched it and what was in it, but sunk in a tar pit, dirtied, corroded, dented, rusted, and lost. We need to be found, dug up, cleaned up, hammered into shape, polished, and restored so that our actual worth might shine. Each of us is at different stages of this restorative process that is God's plan for us.

> The state of our human nature is not endowed with the original health and righteousness possessed by the first man when he was created. On the contrary, we are greatly depraved by sin. Still, that holy inclination to love God above all things remains with us, as does the natural light of reason by which we know that his supreme goodness is lovable above all things. It is impossible for a man who thinks attentively about God, even by natural reason alone, not to feel a certain glow of love. Our nature's secret inclination arouses this glow at the bottom of our hearts. By it, at the first apprehension of the first and supreme object, the will is seized upon and feels itself to be aroused to take complacence in it. (St. Francis de Sales, *TLG*, 1:16)

SCRIPTURE REFLECTION

Read three parables in the Gospel of Luke: The Lost Sheep (15:1–7); the Lost Coin (15:8–10), and the Prodigal Son and his brother (15:11–32).

QUESTIONS FOR REFLECTION

1. What brain change will it take for me to let go of some of the dysfunctional self-image that I am attached to and what do I have to do to make that happen?

2. Why would I cling to a negative understanding of myself?

3. What are the behavioral consequences of my self-understanding?

SUGGESTED ACTIVITIES

Write first-person affirmations for yourself. Base them on biblical texts as a mental therapy to change your attitude, your inner conversation. Your brain is malleable, shaped and reshaped by your thinking. For example:

I am made in God's image (Gen 1:27).

God breathed into me the breath of life (Gen 2:7).

I am the beloved of the Lord (Deut 33:12).

Write affirmations based on the three Scripture passages above and the ones listed below or others that speak to you. Or simply make up your own affirmations. Repeat them regularly to yourself, or get a copy of and listen to my half-hour meditation on *Relaxing in God's Love*, which does it for you.[1]

Deut 7:6ff.	John 15:19
Deut 10:14	John 13:16
2 Chr 9:8	John 14:21
Isa 49:15–16	John 13:1
Isa 60:1	Rom 5:5
Isa 43:4	Rom 5:8
Isa 54:8	Rom 8:35
Isa 54:10	Gal 2:20
Hos 11:1ff.	Gal 5:24
Hos 14:5–6	1 Cor 4:17
Zeph 3:17	Eph 5:2
Ps 17:8	1 Thess 5:5
Ps 41:12–13	1 Thess 1:4
Matt 5:13–14	1 John 3:1
Mark 10:21	1 John 5:19ff.
Mark 9:41	Eph 3:14ff.
John 1:14–19	

NOTES

1. John Graden, *Relaxing in God's Love*, performed by John Graden, DeSales Resources and Ministries, Inc. Stella Niagara, NY. 1-800-782-2270. www.EmbracedbyGod.org.

Chapter 5
The Concept of God

Let us consider when we shall be in possession of the glory of Paradise, how great will be our astonishment on seeing the infinite goodness, the incomprehensible immensity, and the supreme majesty of God, Who has lowered Himself so far as to desire the love of the creatures. If the soul were capable of dying, it would die at the sight of this excessive love, of this immense greatness of its Creator, which has so favored it.

—St. Jane de Chantal, *JSJ*, 252–53

IT'S A MYSTERY

"Hey, Father," the student asked, "how is it that Jesus was born of Mary, but she still remained a virgin?" The priest, who was our religion teacher, obviously not up to the task of plumbing the obvious depths of our questioning, simply said, "It's a mystery. Just believe it." Not very satisfying, we thought. He certainly didn't want to talk about sex, let alone the sex of the Virgin Mary. And we so wanted to talk about sex. "Mystery," it seemed, was the religious cover-all, cop-out response when an adult didn't know the answer or didn't want to talk to us.

Years later, in reading both science and religion, I found the word *mystery* appearing again and again: the *mysteries* of the universe, the *mysteries* of physics in deep space, the *mysteries* of black holes or dark matter, and the *mysteries* of the Trinity, whether it be the birth of Christ, the presence of Jesus in the Eucharist, or his presence in you and me for that matter. "Mystery" was something only partially known, and no matter how much we learned, we opened up as many questions as the answers we received and returned to *mystery*. There is more to know. More evidence is needed. Theory needs ongoing revision.

The same is true in religion, especially with our understanding of God. It is fair to say that we know *something* about God. At least those of us who are believers perceive God as a primary cause behind everything that exists. We also believe that we know *something* about God from the revelations of the Bible. Many of us claim to have experiences that point to an existence beyond material things:

> God, an invisible Spirit
> who makes Godself available to us in images that
>   humans can grasp,
> like the beauty of nature, and relationships,
> the mystery of another person or their creativity,
> the person of Jesus of Nazareth, or the activity of the
>   Holy Spirit
> the transcendence of music,
> or the exquisite ecstasy of human love itself—just to name
>   a few.

In fact, in theology we don't think of mysteries so much as solvable but rather as vast wondrous realities about which there is always more to know, to discover, and to experience. Theology teaches that we can never grasp the total mystery that is God, so we are left with images in our mind that capture *something* of the reality and which we should recognize as an insightful, but partial, and not always literal, image. For example, we read in the Bible, "The Lord is my Shepherd." Does this mean literally that God is a shepherd and I am a lamb? Of course not, but the image is exceedingly helpful in understanding something about God.

IMAGES OF GOD

There might possibly be some real atheists in the world, although it is very hard to be absolutely convinced that something doesn't even exist. Most of us are really either believing agnostics or atheistic agnostics, not positive about the existence of God but leaning one way or the other.

However, being a true *atheist* seems to require an astounding intelligence and a staggering faith in natural science, which by its own definition deals with measurable material phenomena and can little conceive an invisible immaterial God. Science itself would then be the atheist's god. And then believers would see science as just another one of the idols that we have so often projected as God. Such idols can be things that we worship that aren't really God, such as money, sex, fame, youth, success, science, and so on, or they could be false *images* of God that aren't really God either, such as an old man in the sky, an angry accountant, vengeful judge, and the like.

If I had to accept some people's images or concepts of God, I would be an atheist. I would think that no such god exists, and if that god did exist, I would not be interested, let alone in love, with such a god. Whatever my image of God is, it has to be *big* enough for me to dedicate my entire life to. So I wonder what God image some people have rejected. Have they rejected what are basically idols anyhow? Actually, that would be a good start for the spiritual life!

Even if we aren't dealing with a false image of God, an idol, we still may have different true angles on the same mystery. One ancient parable helps us understand how the varied perspectives on a reality are so much larger than just one person can perceive. The parable "The Blind Men and the Elephant," which has variations in many religious traditions of India, describes how six blind men each touch a different part of an elephant, and thus each has his own unique perspective on the elephant's shape. The parable sets up the question that if we can't see something the way some-one else sees it, is it because the other's perception is false or because of human limitations in perceiving?

We should ask ourselves, "What is *my* image of God? Does my current image of God match my level of education, intelli-gence, and life experiences? Am I a functional atheist or agnostic because my image of God is so far beneath my present maturity that I cannot accept it as true? What do I want to let go of, and what do I want to hang onto?"

The Santa Claus image of God is usually apparent when all our prayer is asking God for things and promising to be good so that our wishes are granted. If we get what we asked for, then we think that God answered our prayers. If we didn't get what we asked for, then God didn't answer our prayers. It probably doesn't occur to us that even Santa can indeed say no to our requests. For some people, when this image of God hasn't worked, they simply have "taken their ball and gone home," walking away from faith in God or from any practice of religion.

For some, God is the accountant who keeps track of every little thing we do on a big spreadsheet, which we hope will show more deposits than withdrawals. Perhaps this attitude is more about how we approach relationships, counting the pluses and minuses of our friends' behaviors, than it is about God. Others think of the angry God who can't wait to fry our butts for infrac-tions of his Law. Again, this approach may reflect our own experi-ences with parents, teachers, coaches, or police more than it tells us anything about God. Ask yourself: Are there any elements of these images of God in my consciousness? Do I really need or want to hang onto them?

A popular image of God is that of the micromanager who does everything and controls everything. A woman asks her hus-band in the midst of everything going wrong, "Does God hate us, or what?"—as if God is responsible for everything happening. A man says to me, "Well, after all, God is in charge, isn't that right,

Father?" How do I answer? He expects me to agree, is shocked if I disagree, and is scandalized by my lack of faith and confused if I say, "It depends on just what you mean."

This micromanaging god becomes *responsible* for everything, and we and the rest of the universe responsible for nothing. A drunk driver kills a kid, and people get mad at God. A young mother dies from cancer, and we blame God. People die from a flood, a tornado, an earthquake, a birth defect, and we say God caused it. Is God responsible for any of these things?

We need to consider our personal images of God and how we understand God's presence and working in the world. Our images of God are often so deeply embedded in our psyche that we can become firmly attached to them, convinced that we are right, and not see an alternative. When our image is threatened by life experience, we frequently feel like we are having a faith crisis, and we feel foolish and confused. However, when the old image crumbles, it makes way for the building of a new image that fits better with our new experiences. In the meantime, we can either be excited about adventuring into unknown territory or simply confused.

GOD IS LOVE

When reflecting on images of God, consider the simple descriptive equation: "Beloved, let us love one another, because love is from God; everyone who loves is born of God and knows God. Whoever does not love does not know God, for God is love" (1 John 4:7–8).

God is love. This is the most basic image of God. God loves me because God is love; God is one who loves. How much I am loved isn't dependent upon me and my goodness or foolishness but upon the very nature of God. Love is what God is and what God does. We see Jesus as the image of this invisible God who is love (Col 1:15). In fact, Jesus is such a perfect image of God that we think of him *as* God. If you wonder what God is like, contemplate Jesus in the Bible, especially in the Gospels.

What image of God will also help us to understand how God operates in this natural world that we keep learning more and more about through science? What about creation? What about evolution? What about free will and the problem of evil? Some people claim to have given up faith in God completely because they cannot put together a God of love with the overwhelming evil in the world. How can the image of God as Love make sense of this?

The Frisbee God

Imagine the immensity of the God, who is Love, constantly releasing quanta energy from the divine heart[1] like tossing Frisbees. This energy is saturated, marinated, immersed, imbued, and interpenetrated with the presence, the power, the freedom, the love, the creativity, and the dynamism of God's own self. God sends forth this energy in abundance, as if saying, "Go! Create! Be! Become! Be free! Do! Be responsible for what you do! Love! Develop! Evolve! Quarks, elements, life, consciousness! I love you and am with you and within you in every moment, and it is my energy and power that are enabling your existence and activity. Let's see what you're going to do with what I have given you. My presence, love, and concern will embrace you in everything that happens, no matter what."

This *Frisbee-God* image relates with my experience of God and the universe. God is the primary Lover and Mover but so profligately gives away freedom, power, and control (no power freak, this God) to particles, atoms, molecules, stars, and life, that all creation shares in the immensity of the energy that comes from God. When a chemical reaction occurs, it isn't God doing it, although the impulse of creative power has come from God, but atoms and molecules are interacting as they *will*, and some of this may even be totally random. As stars are born and die, species evolve and become extinct, a human passes a test or murders another person. It isn't God doing these things, although all the power has come from a God so incredibly committed to freedom as to allow all creation itself the latitude to act, while all the time God embraces everything with the providential care and compassion and unimaginable love of the perfect mother and father.

Isn't this what the best mom and dad do with their children? They raise them to be competent, free, and responsible, no longer controlling them or being responsible for them, and loving their children still no matter what they do.

God has an even greater power to make "all things work together for good for those who love God" (Rom 8:28). Like the best Scrabble players who can make championship words out of the oddest combinations of letters, God can take whatever the universe does and bring good out of it. Like the best cooks who search the refrigerator, freezer, and cupboards and concoct a delicious meal, so God is able to do something good with whatever actions and products the universe generates. The ultimate proof of this creative ability of God is found in the crucifixion of the innocent Son of God. This cosmic injustice is flipped on its head and becomes the salvation of all humanity and creation itself. O Happy Fault!

How does this image of God stand up against miracles—things happening with no scientific explanation? Is God micromanaging these events? Or are they an astonishing coincidence? Of course, the God of the universe can do anything God chooses to do and isn't limited by any image whatsoever. Is it God working in and through God's presence within nature—a rather frequent phenomenon—or is God acting from the outside, manipulating nature, also clearly possible? Either way, we can still call it a miracle in that all reality is interactive with God. Therefore, to say that God is in charge depends on different circumstances and meanings.

SEEKING THE TRUE GOD

In Genesis, we see how Jacob wrestles with the man whom he understands later to be the sight of God face-to-face.

> Jacob was left alone; and a man wrestled with him until daybreak....Then the man said, "You shall no longer be called Jacob, but Israel, for you have striven with God and with humans, and have prevailed." Then Jacob asked him, "Please tell me your name." But he said, "Why is it that you ask my name?" And there he blessed him. So Jacob called the place Peniel, saying, "For I have seen God face to face, and yet my life is preserved." (Gen 32:24–30)

Wrestling is clearly an intimate contact sport, requiring strength, cunning, and a willingness to try different maneuvers that respond to the moves of one's wrestling partner. Perhaps that can be a parable for our seeking the face of the God we long to find.

What is not an idol but a *true* image, even if it is only miniscule and partial? (Remember the six blind men touching the elephant. To get a *true*, even limited, perspective on the elephant, the men at least had to be exploring an elephant and not a giraffe.) Exploring a non-God (giraffe) doesn't let us know too much about what God (an elephant) is. To begin to get an accurate picture of God, we have to get close and begin to explore like those blind men. We must be willing to wrestle with our own ideas and experiences. The Bible—most particularly that perfect image of the invisible God, Jesus Christ the Lord—is the standard we can use to see if we are getting closer to an accurate picture of God. Go to Jesus who loves you.

We must hang onto Jesus whom our heart loves, because God has placed that love deep within us. We let go of everything else, every other image, since we'll need both hands and arms to hang onto Jesus, perhaps wrapping our arms and legs around the base of the cross, that mast of the ship that is rockin' and rollin' on stormy seas. We must hold on and never let go.

> Our Lord loves with a most tender love those who are so happy as to abandon themselves wholly to His fatherly care, letting themselves be governed by His divine Providence....All that is required is that they should place all their confidence in Him, and say from their heart: "Into Thy blessed hands I commend my spirit, my soul, my body and all that I have, to do with them as it shall please Thee." (St. Francis de Sales, *SPC*, 23–24)

SCRIPTURE REFLECTION

Jesus said, "Those who love me will keep my word, and my Father will love them, and we will come to them and make our home with them" (John 14:23).

QUESTIONS FOR REFLECTION

1. How can I recognize the image of God that operates in my mind or that of someone else's? How can I respectfully and gently invite further growth?

2. Do I feel uncomfortable and confused crafting an updated image of God for myself? Why or why not?

3. What help do I need to kill or immobilize the idols in my life and be sure that I am seeking the true God?

SUGGESTED ACTIVITIES

1. Ask God in prayer to fill you with the Holy Spirit and ask for insight into God.

2. Create a timeline of your life, and place at various points a few symbols for the various images of God that you've held, for example, such symbols as a Christmas tree for Santa, a gavel for the Judge, and more.

3. Read at least one paragraph from the Gospels every day and see what is revealed about God.

NOTES

1. I use the word *heart* in the biblical sense, which always refers to the deepest center of a being; we use it in that sense when we say, "Let's have a heart-to-heart talk," or "I mean this from the bottom of my heart."

Chapter 6

Success, Failure, and the Need to Be Right

It is a good practice of humility not to study the actions of others save to find out their virtues, for as to their imperfections, as long as we are not in charge of them we must never turn either our eyes or our consideration in that direction.

—St. Francis de Sales, *SPC*, 71

EXPECTATIONS

Because I was the eldest of four, there were often high expectations placed on me as I was growing up. My father, who was a U.S. Army Sergeant with a deep booming voice, corrected me neither harshly nor by punishment, but usually by way of expectations. One day, when I was five, I had my elbows on the kitchen table at supper time. Dad didn't simply tell me to get my elbows off the table, rather he said gently but directly, "Johnny, if you're tired, you can go to bed; otherwise take your elbows off the table. The table is not a bed." The expectation was clear. The next year, when Dad died of leukemia, well-intentioned people said to me that now I would have to be "the man of the house." I grew up hearing how bright my father was and knew that I was expected to do well in school.

In her later years, Mom told me that she always told us just to do our best in school. I'm not sure what she actually said way back then, but I *thought* that I also heard that the goal was for me to be the first in the class. While I did come first several times in my early years in a small inner city Catholic grade school, high school, which required a placement test, found me swimming in a much bigger pond. Suddenly, that same level of success was out of reach. What is your story?

SUCCESS

It isn't hard to see why I have struggled for a long time with my self-worth being tightly attached to my success, at least as I perceived it. I have long tried to detach myself from desperately clinging to accomplishments as the currency of my value. It's so American! It's so masculine!

My remedy has been to untie myself from the debilitating dock of "what I do is what I'm worth"—being a *human doing*—and pushing, rowing, or sailing out to the joyful waters of "who I am is what I'm worth"—being a *human being*.

The things we discussed in chapter 4 about belonging to the God who made me in God's own image, as a holy temple of the Holy Spirit and a member of the body of Christ, are also applicable here. They keep us moving away from that suck-you-dry dock of dwelling only on our perceived successes and failures.

Of course, we *always* try to be successful in what we undertake. To do otherwise would be foolish, and would no doubt undermine our efforts to do something good. However, once we have achieved what we set out to do, the results are no longer ours to control. Perhaps we aren't yet finished, and still have something more we can continue to do to advance the success of our project. However, there comes a point when our part in a venture is completed, and we are left either with enjoying praise, being blamed, or being unrecognized for our labors—possibly a combination of all three. Nevertheless, hanging onto past successes too tightly is to return to that dock of ego, of being a human doing rather than a human being. Certainly we can be happy about our successes in this world, and thank God for them and for the talent that enabled us to be an instrument in God's hand. Apart from your résumé, needing to bring up successes in conversation to see that they get noted by others only serves our self-centered insecurities and indicates how tightly we are still clinging to our earthly doings, instead of focusing on our divine destiny and identity of *being* in union eternally with the Lord, the Awesome One.

FAILURES

Of course, hanging onto our failures creates the same *human doing* problems, and reduces us to what we have done and failed to do. Is it possible to be alive and never fail at anything? It has not been possible for me, although I have sometimes been vain enough to have tried to cover up my failures. For a number of years, I lived with a dear friend in community who was prone to doing spacey things. At supper, he would share some ridiculous thing he did that day. I would think, "Holy mackerel, if I did that, it would be ten years before I'd be telling anybody—that is, unless I had been caught at it." My friend was just humble enough to spill the beans on himself every day. Amazing!

There are certainly sins, failures, and misjudgments in my life that haunt me, but mostly I've been figuring out how to let go of them. Confessors and counselors have been especially helpful in getting me to accept the real me, gifted and flawed at the same time, a sinner, in much need of God's mercy.

In the Bible, there are dozens of imperfect and inadequate sinners that God used to accomplish good work. I found a short list of them online one time, expanded the lines to rhyme, researched the biblical references, and then set them to music. I sang it the first time a few years ago in a talk while I was humorously playing the part of Gideon, who was also inadequate for the job except for God's grace and selection (Judg 6—7).

♫ Biblical Bozos[1]

1. NOAH one time got himself naked drunk	[Gen 9]
And JEREMIAH was too young a punk	[Jer 1]
2. ABRAHAM was way too old to be a father	[Gen 17—21]
LEAH was so ugly then heck why bother	[Gen 29]
3. JOSEPH by his brothers got seriously abused	[Gen 37]
of murder 'n adultery DAVID rightly was accused	[2 Sam 11—12]
4. MOSES murdered, hab a broblem wib his speech	[Exod 2, 4]
ISAIAH had hot lips, streaked naked while he preached	[Isa 6, 20]
5. Long haired SAMSON couldn't keep his hands off wimmin	[Judg 13—16]
JONAH ran from God, found himself with fishes swimming	[Jonah]
6. NAOMI a sad widow, and she had lost her man	[Ruth 1]
RAHAB was a prostitute with one more in the can	[Josh 2]
7. HOSEA loved and married an unrepentant whore	
To image how God still loved us ever more and more	[Hos 1—3]
8. ELIJAH he was persecuted, desired then to die	[1 Kgs 19]
JAMES & JOHN wanted their enemies to fry	[Luke 9:54]
9. JOB he was a rich man who bankrupt lost it all	[Job 1, 2]
ZACCHAEUS was a tax collector, Oh so small	[Luke 19]
10. MARY was a virgin, with none to give her hugs	[Luke 1]
But later JOHN THE BAPTIST in the desert, he ate bugs	[Mark 1]
11. MARTHA fret & fret, about many things she worried	[Luke 10]
PETER three times denied the Christ, then he scurried	[Mark 14]
12. The DISCIPLES all slept, when they were s'pposed to pray	[Mark 14]
SAMARITAN WOMAN divorced again, with another one she lay	[John 4]
13. PAUL was so religious, Christians made him see red	[Acts 9]
And LAZARUS? His problem was that he was dead	[John 11]

Spoken: So what's your problem? Whatever God wants you to do, you can do it.

Can we eventually let go of our failures or must they cling to us like a ball and chain? Can we throw ourselves upon the mercy of God, who loves us so much and looks on his children with the delight of parents looking in on their sleeping child? (Ps 127:2). I suppose that our inability to forget our failures helps to make us humble, and I really need that help. Hopefully, it doesn't paralyze us from doing good things according to God's grace. We do have a choice on which things to focus our attention. The most helpful thing is to keep our eyes fixed on Jesus, not our own accomplishments or failures. What do you pay most attention to?

Sherlock Holmes and Dr. Watson were going camping. They pitched their tent under the stars and went to sleep. Sometime in the middle of the night Holmes woke Watson up and said: "Watson, Watson, look up at the sky, and tell me what you see." Watson replied: "I see millions and millions of stars." Holmes said: "And what do you deduce from that?" Watson replied: "Well, if there are millions of stars, and if even a few of those have planets, it's quite likely there are some planets like Earth out there. And if there are a few planets like Earth out there, there might also be life." And Holmes said: "Watson, you idiot, it means that somebody has stolen our tent."

(Submitted by Geoff Anandappa for a Wikipedia contest of funniest jokes)

THE NEED TO BE RIGHT

If I didn't think I was right, I'd change my mind until I was right! I wouldn't hang onto something that I thought was wrong. Would you? The problem occurs when I *think* I am right, and logically then, others who disagree must be wrong. The assumption is that I *know* what is right.

One day, a man came up to me after Mass, and in a voice that I understood to preface some disagreement with something I had said, unapologetically declared, "Father, pardon me, but I tell it like it is, and…." I immediately wanted to genuflect in front of him as a god who could tell just how reality is. "My Lord and my God," came to mind. Now in fairness to him, what he probably meant was that he spared no words in saying just what he thought, so forgive him if it was offensive. But that is not what he said: "I tell it like it is." After I heard him, I realized that I must come across like that a good deal of the time. Years ago, Mom stopped me one time, and very privately suggested that in my various pontifications, it would serve me well to insert some conditional adverbial words, phrases, or clauses, like "perhaps," or "maybe," or "it seems to me," or "as far as I can tell," or "I was taught that…," or "in my not so humble opinion." Otherwise, she added, you sound like a know-it-all who looks down at any disagreement or other perspective as ignorant. Ouch! No doubt, she herself had been prompted to feel that way when I had been talking, and probably enough times that she noticed a pattern. I have to let go of that underlying arrogance that is overly impressed with my intelligence and education.

My impatience and irritation, I have found, are also related to this arrogance. I operate as if the universe revolves around me.

- The red traffic lights ought to be green when I'm in a hurry. Doesn't it know?

- The car shouldn't break down while I am on the way to the airport.

- The computer ought to do what I want it to do.

- The grocery store checkout line should not take forever.

- The mobile phone shouldn't simply lose a call for no apparent reason.

- The kids ought to know better than to act like kids when I have a headache.

Eventually, I realized that I am not God; I am not in charge. My expectations don't matter all that much to the rest of the world. The rhythm of the cosmos is not mine to establish, nor is it yours to establish. Rather than getting frustrated by my inability to control and manipulate reality, can I learn to approach everything that happens as another part of the adventure?

For a few weeks, I recited the mind-altering mantra, "I am not God. I am not God. I am not God." Furthermore, laughter is the only appropriate punctuation after "I am not God (laugh). What was I thinking?" Consequently, my first response to a "change in plans" brought on by circumstances beyond my control is no longer impatience, but a creative refiguring of what to do next. Periodically, I return to that same basic mental therapy, which has become a spiritual exercise that I often need to repeat. Because the old thought programs may be so ingrained, it is necessary to reinforce constantly the newer positive thought habit so that it may dominate my responses.

I have a good friend, whom I'll call Mark. At one point a couple of years ago when his wife left him, she called him a self-righteous jerk. That hurt. However, a few months later, he found that he called *himself* a self-righteous jerk as an excuse for something. We both laughed. On another occasion, I made reference to the same thing and said, "After all, you are a self-righteous jerk, you know." We both laughed again. I suggested, "We should start a club for people like us, and I get to be the first member since I am the senior member, and you the second." Consequently, Mark and I are the charter members of the SRJ club. We developed a club membership card and a way to invite others to recognize themselves and own up to belonging to the SRJ club:

SRJC *Self-Righteous Jerk Club*

A long-time member myself, I have been asked to offer you a **premier membership** since you are so eminently qualified. Your acknowledgment is usually the most painful part.

Your name_____

Our premier membership in the SRJ club is a step toward letting go of the need to be right and hanging onto the reality of seeing ourselves as we are. Perhaps it's a poor attempt to be poor in spirit. However, it certainly makes us laugh at ourselves, which is healthy.

> "Blessed are the poor in spirit, for theirs is the kingdom of heaven." (Matt 5:3)

SCRIPTURE REFLECTION

[Jesus] also told this parable to some who trusted in themselves that they were righteous and regarded others with contempt: "Two men went up to the temple to pray, one a Pharisee and the other a tax collector. The Pharisee, standing by himself, was praying thus, 'God, I thank you that I am not like other people: thieves, rogues, adulterers, or even like this tax collector. I fast twice a week; I give a tenth of all my income.' But the tax collector, standing far off, would not even look up to heaven, but was beating his breast and saying, 'God, be merciful to me, a sinner!' I tell you, this man went down to his home justified rather than the other; for all who exalt themselves will be humbled, but all who humble themselves will be exalted." (Luke 18:9–14)

QUESTIONS FOR REFLECTION

1. What is the basis of my self-worth?

2. Is it real or even healthy to let go completely of our failures or successes? Why?

3. What mental thought habits will be helpful for me to rewrite?

SUGGESTED ACTIVITIES

1. Ask God in prayer to fill you with the Holy Spirit so that you may see yourself as you really are. This requires strength and courage, and maybe even a sense of humor.

2. Thank God for every success and ask for mercy for every failure.

3. Write an appropriate corrective mantra that provides you with a realistic thought habit.

NOTES

1. "Biblical Bozos" written by John Graden © 2010. Sung to the tune of "Mama Loves Short'nin Bread."

Chapter 7
Friendships, Relationships, and Forgiveness

Our sweet Savior had thoughts of love even for his execution-
ers, giving us an example beyond all that we could ever have
imagined, since He made excuses for those who mocked and
crucified Him in their barbarous fury, seeking for motives
whereby to obtain for them His Father's forgiveness at the very
moment of their sin and outrage. Oh, how miserable are we
poor children of earth! For we can scarcely forget an injury,
even long after we have received it! But he who shall prevent[1]
his neighbor with the blessings of sweetness, will be the most
perfect imitator of Our Lord.

—St. Francis de Sales, *SPC,* 66

FRIENDSHIPS

Friendship is one of the most necessary and beautiful things in
life. Consider the following paragraph of a letter from Francis de
Sales, bishop of Geneva, to his best friend, the Baronne de Chantal
(the future St. Jane de Chantal).

> I will not try and say how full my heart is for you, but I
> will say that it is full beyond compare; and this affection
> is whiter than snow, purer than the sun: that is why I
> have given it free rein since you left me, letting it have its
> way. Oh, how impossible to tell, my Lord and God, how

consoling it will be to love one another in heaven in this full sea of charity, when even these little brooklets of love give us so much! (St. Francis de Sales, *LST*, 95)

For Francis de Sales, our earthly friendships give us just a peek of what heaven will be like. There is a huge industry on how to make and keep friends. So I am not going to try to duplicate, nor even summarize it here. Let's rather focus on the spirituality of friendship, particularly hanging on and letting go.

Some friends we make stay close for life. What a blessing these friends are! They give us a glimpse of heaven: ongoing relationship, support, and unconditional love. These friends enable us to persevere, to strive, and to survive the hardest of times. It isn't always what they do for us, but rather that they are simply best friends. Who are these friends for you?

There are school or neighborhood friends, who might grow in different directions and lose contact. They have mostly shared a past, and may or may not still click as friends who spend regular time together. These friends were important in teaching us about relationships.

When I was in early grade school and still a skinny little boy without a dad (before I started getting bigger and bulkier), I had one especially good friend, Danny, who taught me what a friend's loyalty is really about. He stuck right with me, and was always my friend. Did you have a friend like that? Who were your earliest friends, and what did you learn in the relationships?

There are a few friends, whom I regard as "heart-friends"— when your heart and soul resonate in some inexplicable way, no matter the time and distance that separate you. Time, distance, lack of contact, or some issue lurking in the consciousness of one or the other can separate people so that they are literally unable to be together, even if both are still alive. I have a short list of people whom I miss with all my heart and would rejoice the instant I could find a way to be together. Furthermore, there are times that

I really have a longing to see, to talk with, to walk with, and to hug them. However, it is not to be, at least not for now. So I am left only with rejoicing at having had the connection, the experience of someone with whom my heart beat together. I have been enriched and am more human for the experience, even if it hasn't continued as an active relationship today.

Let us now look at those friends we have and sometimes have to let go.

LETTING GO IN DEATH

My Lebanese maternal grandfather, Joseph A. Haddad, whom we always called *Jiddo* (Arabic for grandfather), lived to be ninety-four years old, and died in 1974. He outlived many of his friends and cronies, and understandably felt lonely at times for their company.

One of the ballad-like songs on Elton John's third album, *Tumbleweed Connection* (1970), is called "Talking Old Soldiers," in which an old soldier speaks about the young men he knew in the war and who have all died. He is left with the graveyard as his only friend.[2] I spent many hours listening to this song and reflecting on my Jiddo's experience of growing old enough to lose many relatives and friends. It is certainly true that the longer we live, the more people we have known will die. Some people, even children, don't even have to get old to experience this feeling. Consider the deaths and the loss of relationships as a result of the Holocaust, the Rwandan genocide, the events of 9/11, school shootings, or any number of humanly perpetrated acts of violence and accidents, not to mention the tragedies of nature.

Inevitably, there are times when reality simply forces us to let go of someone close to us. The most difficult people to lose are our children. St. Jane de Chantal lost two of her first newly born children, and she herself outlived three of the next four who survived childhood. She was twenty-nine with four little children when she also lost her husband, and later, she lost her spiritual director, Francis de Sales, who was like another part of her heart. I can only imagine the pain some parents go through in the loss of their children. My own mother, Dorothy, had a strong fear of this loss, and forbade any of her four children to die before she did. Although we didn't have much say, God evidently honored her request. Mom eventually died at the age of eighty-seven, before any of her children.

Nevertheless, some people cling so tenaciously to those who have died that it is difficult for them to get on with life. This raises the question—*how much* remembering and mourning are *too* much? Should we keep the deceased's room and clothes just as they were, and if so, for how long? Twenty-five years? Should we speak of the deceased only in the present tense? Some have analyzed and noted the stages of mourning—denial, anger, bargaining, depression, acceptance—but these stages aren't necessarily part of everyone's experience, nor are they a required process.

When my mother died, I fully expected to crash into an emotional wall at some point. She was always such an intimate part of my psyche, and indeed my greatest supporter in life, especially once my father died after my sixth birthday. I remember my feelings when my Jiddo died, and so when Mom died, I thought that it would be ten times more crushing, but strangely it wasn't. What was going on here? Was I in denial, or had I become cold and hardened by life? I didn't go through those classic grieving stages.

In discussing this feeling with my brother, my sisters, and others, it appears that some of us have lived long enough, dealing with the reality of our own and other's inevitable deaths, that we have developed an interior resilience—learning that death is normal and to be expected. Mom herself taught us this in her willingness to speak often about when she would be gone and in her often repeated sayings from her Arabic language tradition. If a sentence had a future tense verb, she would conclude with the words *God willing* (sometimes even in Arabic):

"I'll see you tonight after school, God willing."

"We will be back by four o'clock, God willing."

"He will graduate at the end of the semester, *In shaa Allah.*"

This simple expression taught us to make plans and have expectations, but to know that something else may intervene, and that life is unpredictable and even terminal. Of course, the older you get, the more you become aware of the reality of death. Only a fool would ignore such an inevitable reality—awareness of one's own death, as well as the death of others. It is easier to deal with the reality when it is an older person dying rather than someone young. It is reasonable to *expect* older people to die before young people. However, that expectation sometimes doesn't match the reality.

So, how do we let go of and how do we hang onto the people we love?

- Know that we or they may be the first to die, unless we die together. Mom and I spoke of this numerous times together. We've got to get this reality through our thick skulls and cloudy consciousness.

- Make the most of the moments we have through communication and presence.

- Be there for the person you love, even in their last moments, if possible.

- Regularly say what you really want to say to each other, and do what you really want to do together while there is time.

66

- Keep the memories and the conversation alive after the person you love has died. (I talk to Mama often, although I wonder whether or not she can see everything I am doing!)

- Have a tradition of visiting and praying at the grave site.

- Celebrate the great gift of life that the person has been to us. For example, my sister, Jeanne, has started a tradition of inviting family and friends on the weekend nearest Mom's birthday and preparing a feast of her Lebanese recipes. I like that, a lot!

Suicide

No doubt, one of the most difficult losses in death occurs when someone we know has committed suicide, and most painfully, of course, when the person is not only someone we know but someone we love deeply. The suffering is traumatic, evoking a range of conflicting feelings, many of which are not very helpful.

Immediately following the shock, blaming, and scapegoating, we wrestle frequently with the "why" and "if only." It is difficult to accept and understand the mystery of not knowing what was or wasn't going on in a person's mind that hurt so powerfully as to overcome the instinct to survive—at least for a few deadly and critical moments. As St. Paul said, "I do not understand my own actions. For I do not do what I want, but I do the very thing I hate" (Rom 7:15).

It is helpful to stop blaming anyone, including yourself, and certainly also the deceased. Not only is such blame fruitless, but it can be deeply self-centered.

Love and presence are needed in the face of such a tragic mystery. Hug more than talk; be present more than offer answers, and encourage others to do the same and avoid the blaming.

Rather than obsessing and hanging onto the trauma, sometimes for far too long—even lifetimes—hand the person over to the all-loving hands of the merciful Jesus. Certainly, weep when needed and gently let the deceased be at rest, and the pain be ended—both theirs and yours.

LETTING GO OF HURTS

With age, there is more that I forget; not just where I laid my calendar or mobile phone, why I came into a room, or the meeting I have tonight, but also people I really want to remember. I wish that I could forget some of the things I've done and said, and some of the things that have been done or said by others. That seems to be one of the things God can do that I am not very good at—picking which things to forget:

> Thus says the LORD, your Redeemer, the Holy One of Israel:...I am He who blots out your transgressions for my own sake, and I will not remember your sins. (Isa 43:14, 25)

Speaking of forgetting, I often recall a story of a priest having a vision of God, although he isn't really sure whether it is God, or perhaps a dream or an illusion. So he asks God, "If you are really God, then tell me what the worst sin is that I ever committed." God hesitates, thinks for a long moment before saying, "I forgot." It was then that the priest knew the vision was authentic. The all-powerful God is able to forget!

Don't you wish that you could forget your worst sins as well as all the things in life that have hurt and left you with scars, especially inside? I wish I could forget those hurtful things that somebody else said or did that I have remembered for decades, and that are challenging to forgive. I am always working on forgiveness, but I constantly find little pockets of anger and hurt left over after many years. This applies to memories of my own sins as well as what I perceive to be the sins of others. Knowing better than to hang onto these hurts, I am still a work in progress.

For example, what if you strayed too close to a dart board and caught a "dart in the heart." Perhaps it was thrown at you deliberately, aiming to really hurt you. Perhaps it was tossed carelessly, or by someone whose aim was as bad as when drunk. Perhaps you just unknowingly got in the way. Perhaps it was completely an accident. Perhaps you even did it to yourself. Regardless, you've got a dart in the heart and the pain is motivating some action. It is safe to say that the dart has to come out. Either we yank it out right then and there, or if we suspect possible complications or bleeding, we go and get the help we need to have it taken out safely and the wound treated so as to promote healing and avoid infection, perhaps even getting a tetanus shot. We would certainly not allow the dart to continue infecting and hurting us, just so that we could go around and tell everyone how unfair it is that we have been stabbed.

Of course, the above scenario is ludicrous, and yet that's what we mentally and emotionally tend to do when we have been hurt inside. We often have a tendency to hang onto the hurt and remember it. We irritate it more and keep the pain alive. It would be wonderful if we could select the memory and delete it as easily as we do on the computer. We need to let go of the anger and hurt, simply because they are poisonous, toxic. The results of people hanging onto these wounds for a long time are both sad and ugly.

In my efforts to let go of these hurts, I soak my thoughts in mercy, trying to reframe and reinterpret them, minimizing the injurious scenes. When all else fails, I simply place my wounded heart as it is (self-centered, self-pitying, and self-important) on the altar:

"Lord, take my heart, make it yours, heal it of its wounds, make it more like your heart. Teach me to love and forgive as you do."

I've got to confess that I haven't done this just once, but very frequently. It is not like a magic formula—some *"hocus pocus"*—that suddenly changes everything. "Yippee, I've done it." It is more like a soaking prayer, which needs to happen over and over, like once a day maybe, or as often as possible. It is like some of the daily rituals such as brushing my teeth or moisturizing dry skin. Doing them once isn't enough; it is necessary that these little rituals become part of my lifestyle if they are going to have an effect. Letting go of hurtful things is a gradual process and a daily practice.

Dear God, when we see our neighbor, created to the image and likeness of God, should we not say to one another, "Stop, do you see this created being, do you see how it resembles the Creator?" Should we not cast ourselves upon him, caress him, and weep over him with love? Should we not give him a thousand, thousand blessings? Why so? For love of him? No indeed, for we cannot know whether in himself he is "worthy of love or hate." Why so? It is for love of God who made him in his own image and likeness and therefore capable of sharing in his goodness in grace and glory. I say it is for love of God, from whom he is, whose he is, by whom he is, in whom he is, for whom he is, whom he resembles in a most particular manner. For this reason, the love of God not only often commands love of neighbor but it produces such love and even pours it into man's heart as its resemblance and image. Just as man is God's image, so the sacred love of man for man

is the true image of a heavenly love of man for God.
(St. Francis de Sales, *TLG*, X:11)

HANGING ONTO THE POSITIVES

Hanging onto the life-giving memories, the affirmations, the expressions of love, and the really beautiful things, and letting those memories get absorbed by our inner consciousness through journaling or scrapbooking are ways not to forget the love, affection, and the beauty of life. Since I regard all beauty as the tiniest glimpse of God, I regularly need to immerse myself in what I call "beauty therapy." This involves being mindful of beautiful places, music, art, people, stars, shores and waves, mountains, and moments of love and delight. Using my imagination, I recall pictures and sounds from my travel or from books and films for meditation. One place I regularly go to is the Last Supper, where I am the "disciple whom Jesus loved" and can lean on Jesus and feel loved. Frequently I say nothing, but meditate on the following verse:

"One of his disciples—the one whom Jesus loved—was reclining next to [Jesus]." (John 13:23)

SCRIPTURE REFLECTION

Pleasant speech multiplies friends,
and a gracious tongue multiplies courtesies.
Let those who are friendly with you be many,
but let your advisers be one in a thousand.
When you gain friends, gain them through testing,
and do not trust them hastily.
For there are friends who are such when it suits them,
but they will not stand by you in time of trouble.

And there are friends who change into enemies,
and tell of the quarrel to your disgrace.
And there are friends who sit at your table,
but they will not stand by you in time of trouble.
When you are prosperous, they become your second
    self,
and lord it over your servants;
but if you are brought low, they turn against you,
and hide themselves from you.
Keep away from your enemies,
and be on guard with your friends.
Faithful friends are a sturdy shelter:
whoever finds one has found a treasure.
Faithful friends are beyond price;
no amount can balance their worth.
Faithful friends are life-saving medicine;
and those who fear the Lord will find them.
Those who fear the Lord direct their friendship
    aright,
for as they are, so are their neighbors also." (Sir 6:5–17)

QUESTIONS FOR REFLECTION

1. Who are the friends of my past for whom I can be very grateful?

2. Who are my current friends, whose friendship I really want to continue to cultivate?

3. Which past memories, lingering in anger and hurt, need healing?

4. How can I practice a serious beauty therapy?

SUGGESTED ACTIVITIES

1. Create a list of friends in your life, and keep adding to it as more come to mind, becoming more aware and thankful for the part they have played in your life.

2. Place your wounded heart on the altar or directly into the Sacred Heart of Jesus.

3. Practice a letting go prayer: sitting with fists clenched, hold on, and only slowly and gradually open your hands and fingers and raise them up, giving flight to whatever you were clenching.

4. Create in your mind a library of beauty: pictures, memories, sounds—some places where you can go for beauty therapy.

NOTES

1. The translation is the old usage of the word *prevent*, meaning "to do something ahead of time" or "to anticipate it."

2. Elton John, "Talking Old Soldiers" Lyrics, MetroLyrics (http://www.metrolyrics.com/talking-old-soldiers-lyrics-elton-john.html).

Chapter 8

The Gift of Sexuality

As soon as you are conscious of being tempted, follow the example of children when they see a wolf or bear out in the country. They immediately run to the arms of their father or mother or at least call to them for help or protection. Turn in the same way to God and implore his mercy and help.

—St. Francis de Sales, *IDL*, IV, 7

MADE FROM DIRT
BUT NOT NECESSARILY DIRTY

Sexuality is a wonderful gift from God, through which we participate in the creative act of new life. It is a sacred sharing in the universe's given power to reproduce itself. Unfortunately, many of us grew up with a rather negative Victorian-American approach to sex and sexuality, which we inherited from our Pilgrim and Puritan ancestors. Even mild sexual jokes were, and still are considered as "dirty" jokes, or minimally, off-color. The entire topic was regarded as one of dirt, guilt, and shame, indeed not to be spoken of by "religious" people, except in the confessional.

There is no doubt to this very day, especially with an older penitent in the reconciliation room, that confessing "impure thoughts" always means sexual thoughts. However, is a sexual thought automatically an impure thought? Is it a dirty thought? I suppose if sex is dirty, then any thought of it would be too. Did

Jesus, who was without sin, ever have a sexual thought or feeling? And if so, was it dirty?

> Since, then, we have a great high priest who has passed through the heavens, Jesus, the Son of God, let us hold fast to our confession. For we do not have a high priest who is unable to sympathize with our weaknesses, but we have one who in every respect has been tested as we are, yet without sin. Let us therefore approach the throne of grace with boldness, so that we may receive mercy and find grace to help in time of need. (Heb 4:14–16)

Could Jesus be human and never have a sexual thought, feeling, or urge? Didn't he have the same organs and hormones as we do? Was Jesus a sexual being? Am I being irreverent by even asking these questions? If Jesus was/is fully human, and tempted in every way, yet without sin, then there has to be a way to be a sexual being without it being a sin.

THE ACT OF SEX

Once I was giving a talk on sexuality and one of the participants asked whether I was qualified or experienced enough to give the talk. "Have you ever had sex?" he finally asked. I answered, "Yes…(long pause), I have always had sex. At the time I was born (before ultrasounds), the nurse said, 'Mrs. Graden, it's a boy!' and then they marked the chart and put 'male' indicating the sex of the newborn." I guess I have been a sexual being since those first X and Y chromosomes began to determine how I would develop in the womb. It is how God made me, and I want to be that very well. (I should confess that I had set up that young man to ask me that question, in order to make the point.)

The moral guidance I grew up with seemed to prefer me being neuter and wasn't willing or able to discuss what it means to be "sexual" as a human person. In the examination of conscience books of my youth, mortal sins (deadly or serious sins) were listed in UPPER CASE letters, and literally every action listed under the sixth and ninth commandments was in upper case, including even touching yourself impurely. First, I was scared to death; then I was intrigued by the forbidden fruit; then I had a bad case of V.D., as in virginal depression, and then I wondered whether I was going to die from the white stuff that came out of my body. Finally, I went to the library only to discover that ejaculation was normal for a male and occurred in sexual intercourse, so I presumed it wasn't going to kill me if it happened when there was no woman present. The V.D. returned again, and I fervently wished to be seduced by some sexpot so that I could both have the sex and not be entirely responsible for it. As a sixth grader, I was alternately going to heaven or hell depending on which day of the week it was or whether I had enough courage to grab Fr. Jerry again on the way into Mass for a quick confession. Mercifully, he said, "Thank God for the grace of a good confession. Say three Hail Mary's." I was always greatly relieved that he chose not to talk further about it. On the other hand, I probably would have benefitted from someone who was willing to talk with me about this topic.

LUST AND LOVE

In those days, it seemed like everything about sex was Sin. Sin. Sin. In fact, when we asked for God's mercy for being a sinner, I assumed everybody was talking about sex, and, as a matter of fact, they frequently were. Ah, but then came that sociological phenomenon called the sexual revolution! Soon, everything was permissible, even if for the "unenlightened" it was still illegal and frowned upon by the square set. Sex was fun! It was normal. Birds did it, bees did it. Anything between consenting individuals was supposed to be natural and even healthy, expressive, and loving. As long as it was fun and nobody got hurt. The pendulum had swung from one extreme to the other. When it came to sex, we were unable to deal with any nuances. It was either *all* sin, or all *OK*.

Surely, there is a way to sort out our experiences and actions and take a look at what is clearly not so good, what is better, and what is best. Here, some gentleness and a close and careful look at our experiences would be helpful. It was once while in the confessional, praying with a struggling older person of fairly high values and sensitivity, that a new image occurred to me:

> **The Setting**: My first college degree was in biology. I was teaching high school biology and genetics. We were working with fruit flies, which are relatively easy to study because in a matter of a few weeks you can be dealing with several generations, and noting the inheritance of eye color and shape for example. You keep the flies in small glass containers with some fruit food for them, both to eat and in which to lays their eggs.
>
> **The Image**: To be able to inspect them closely and separate them for whatever purpose, we would put a little ether on the cotton above the container, wait for the flies to be put to sleep by the ether, and carefully pour them out onto a glass plate under a magnifier. Then, working fast before they awoke and flew away, you would separate males and females, and sort the ones with certain characteristics. Now to do this work, you cannot use your fingers, which would crush or injure them, but a fine artists' paint brush to move them around delicately, separating and put them into new dwellings according to the plan of your experiment. It

was precisely this magnified and delicate sorting with the artist's brush that is the image that came to mind.

Following his confession, I ask my penitent to review his or her sexual experiences and to place them on a two foot horizontal line scaled from 0 to 100 stretching from left to right. Then, locate the experiences that were clearly bad, immature, or selfish toward one end of the line (zero), and those that were much better and loving toward the other end (100), and to pay attention to the details that made the experiences at each end of the scale different. My advice is always to move your sexuality in the direction of the good, the best.

Lust is at one end of the line, and Love at the other. They differ radically and are not the same thing. Sex, sexuality, lust, and love can be distinguished from each other, not all melted into one ball of wax. Following are some differences that I have noted. Perhaps you can add more:

LUST	LOVE
Attraction to beauty/desire	Attraction to beauty/desire
Wild out-of-order desire	Desire for mutual love and creating life
Instinctive/natural/animal	Instinctive/natural/animal & spiritual
Dirty and devilish luscious fruit	Natural power for creative loving
Can't wait to take	Can't wait to give
Desire to possess	Desire to please
Satisfy my urgings	Live for the other
Use the other for my pleasure	Put myself at the pleasure of the other
Potential for great harm and violence	Encouraging and building up the other

LUST	LOVE
Others are different available sexual commodities	The other is a unique person I love
Partners as arbitrary playthings	We are part of the body of Christ
If no one is available, just satisfy myself	Alone is longing for union with the other
Repeatedly reinforces my self-centeredness	Calls me out of myself
Seeing persons in terms of what they can do for me	Seeing persons as precious gift
Training for abusive narcissism	The school of other-centered love
Dirty	Pure

In his General Audience of October 8, 1980, Pope John Paul II concluded his analysis of adultery in the heart by observing that it is an attitude of a man toward a woman (or vice versa) that reduces the communion of persons to satisfaction of an instinct. One may be guilty of this attitude toward one's own spouse.[1] He did not mean that there should be no sexual desires or thoughts in marriage, but that it should always be directed toward love and not toward lust, which always and everywhere is the sinful use of the fire that is sexuality. Fire can be phenomenal when it is under control and in the right place—in the furnace of a basement, at a power plant, atop a candle in a dark room, at a campsite—but when out of control, it can be injurious, destructive, explosive, all-consuming, and fatal. The same can be said of sexuality. I don't want to let go of being sexual. It is how God has made me. However, I do want to keep purifying all my drives and desires and directing them to God, to Love itself.

SEXUAL DESIRES

So what are sexual thoughts? Finding someone attractive sexually and wondering what it would be like having sex with them? Being struck by the attractive beauty of another person's body? Feeling stimulated mentally, imaginatively, emotionally, and even physically? This is normal and natural for the human species. It clearly is a "sexual cue" that gets us moving on that track that extends from the depths of lust to the heights of love. Some may see this sexual cue as a temptation; others may immediately think of it as a sin. In fact, it's an opportunity to thank God for being sexual, and to learn how to direct this incredible internal spiritual and physical force toward love. It's a time to laugh at my thoughts and become aware of my thoughts and feelings; to praise God, the maker of such beauty; to realize the dignity of the other person; and to laugh again, for the other person may hardly know or even care whether I exist.

> Lord, I am such a creature of the earth and still very
> self-centered. Lord, have mercy.

Then turn to something else and let your feelings wash over you. By making this first response to your sexual cue a habit, you can eventually relax with your human sexuality. You are not an angel, and there is no need to be embarrassed.

From my experience in the confessional, I've learned that sexual issues are not limited to young people, although they have higher hormonal levels, stronger drives, and less experience for the most part than older people.

Certainly, there are times when I have felt it appropriate to instruct a person that they must stop what they have been doing sexually. It is somewhat parallel to an alcoholic intervention, in which the situation for a person has reached such damaging levels for themselves and/or someone else that the advice to stop immediately is warranted. We then work out a plan to end the damaging behavior or affair:

1. Break off the relationship completely or only be together in public.

2. Stop the sexting (phone texting with sexual content).

3. Get professional help.

4. Turn yourself in.[2]

There is a DeSales Oblate tradition, which in French is called *couper court*, which means "cut it short," and originates from Mother Mary de Sales Chappuis (1793–1875), a Sister of the Visitation of Holy Mary. Cut short the behavior, cut short the temptation, cut short the self-pity, cut short the excess self-attention, and direct your thoughts and feeling toward something else, preferably God. Distract yourself in some way so that the temptation might pass. Intervene and redirect your thoughts and behaviors.

There is no doubt that much evil has been motivated by sexual desire and behavior, and it is a tragic reality that something so beautiful and sacred should be used not for love, but for lust.

Any sexual activity can quickly become genital. It's best to *stop* it before it gets started at all, or certainly as soon as possible, if its full expression is not appropriate. Sex is a powerful fire in the engine, especially for a person who is hungering for love, affection, and acceptance, and is hardwired for it with the software already downloaded. Certainly, the number of unwed pregnancies is indicative of its power.

Masturbation and Pornography

Men and sometimes women come to me to confess that sex and masturbation have been a longtime issue for them, even though they are married. There is often the feeling of guilt, shame, and embarrassment. So I ask, "Since what you have tried hasn't worked very well, are you willing to try a different approach? I cannot guarantee that it will work right away like some magic pill, but I think it is worth a try. Are you willing?"

In most cases, there is a repeated habitual loop and brain pattern that have long been established consisting of an initial sexual cue, followed by anticipation, lustful thoughts, excitement, orgasmic pleasure, and then guilt with temporary but no lasting satisfaction. Finally, there's the need to repeat the process as soon as the human biology will allow it. What can we do to interrupt this loop? I want to turn it upside down and make any sexual cues that would initiate this cycle into a cue for prayer, as suggested earlier, with sexual thoughts.

For penance, I suggest *kneeling* before the Blessed Sacrament and thanking God for the gift of sexuality, for the feelings, the orgasm, and for being sexual and not neuter. If applicable, the person can thank God for the gift of being able to have children. Then I suggest that the person ask God for help in using their sexual gift in a more holy way. Furthermore, I recommend that the person do the same thing every time the sexual cue presents itself. Instead of the person's usual ritual, create a new one that interrupts the usual pattern.

Now, in dealing with internet pornography and masturbation, let's see if we can create some defense lines mentally and habitually.

1. Remember that on the internet, "www" stands for the *world wide web*. Being on the internet is far from private or secret no matter how much it may seem like it is. In fact, numerous marketers are noting what you're interested in so they can sell you more.

2. Since bedtime is frequently an occasion for the sexual cue, write for yourself a really intimate prayer for when

you first awaken and one for just before you fall asleep. (There are some samples in the next chapter, but it has to be your words and has to come straight from your own heart.) Maybe you may also need a prayer during the night if you are awake often during the night.

3. Go to confession as often as possible so that you can start again, and not claim, "Oh well, since I've done it once I may as well do it a whole bunch more times until it's out of my system—all before I go to confession again." You simply want to get back on course as soon as you can.

4. Take advantage of any periods of disgust with your behavior by destroying and throwing away anything you have that is part of your behavior: pornography, toys, and the like. For now you're making a clean start and you want your actions to be as clear as your intention. And you want to create a wider and wider time gap between these behaviors so that you might more readily see that you don't really need them.

5. Learn about the porn industry and the huge amounts of money involved in selling and reducing women, men, and children to sexual commodities. Notice the prevalence today of the modern slavery of the sex trade. Do you want to make this one of your charities?

6. Think about the fact that we usually get good at what we practice. Ask yourself, "What do I wish to present to the Lord as a response to the gifts he has given me?"

7. Recall that you are literally creating your thinking habits, your behaviors, and your character by what you repeatedly choose to focus on. Does porn create the kind of brain you choose to have?

8. Distract yourself in any way you can, especially with prayer.

We must cultivate and nourish wants and desires for what is truly good whenever we can, because our decisions and behaviors emerge from our preconscious brain based on those desires and wants.

When we allow the growth of desires or wants for what is less than good or even evil, we further program our preconscious brain for these behaviors, and the addiction and enslavement process is well on its way.

If we want to be free to choose what is good, we have to form and become slaves to good habits. Otherwise, we become slaves of every impulse, brain chemistry, and cultural conditioning. As St. Paul reminds us, "Now that you have been freed from sin and enslaved to God, the advantage you get is sanctification. The end is eternal life" (Rom 6:22).

A Prayer

Thank you, Lord, for my sexuality.
I am glad to be attracted to people.
I am delighted that I am drawn to love, and that my
    sexuality is the first level of the invitation to notice
    and love someone outside myself.
It is a powerful force calling me to intimate union
    with others and ultimately with you, my God.
So often, I don't invest and use what you give me very
    well, even sometimes very badly. Lord, have mercy.
I know that you love me, even in my self-centered
    blindness.
I am yours, and so often I am blind in my own
    concerns.
Make me more and more yours.

SCRIPTURE REFLECTION

My beloved is mine and I am his;
he pastures his flock among the lilies.

Upon my bed at night
I sought him whom my soul loves;
I sought him, but found him not;
I called him, but he gave no answer.
"I will rise now and go about the city,
in the streets and in the squares;
I will seek him whom my soul loves."
I sought him, but found him not.
The sentinels found me,
as they went about in the city.
"Have you seen him whom my soul loves?"
Scarcely had I passed them,
when I found him whom my soul loves.
I held him, and would not let him go. (Song 2:16, 3:1–4a)

QUESTIONS FOR REFLECTION

1. Which experiences of sexuality do I want to let go of? What do I want to hang onto?

2. Are there parts of this chapter that I agree with or take issue with?

3. Has my experience of sexuality been a call to a love beyond myself?

4. Are any of the skills referred to in this chapter helpful to me?

SUGGESTED ACTIVITIES

1. Imagine a line where you can place the love experiences in your life at one end and the lust experiences at the other as earlier described in the chapter.

2. Try lying face down on the floor in humble prayer before the Lord. If you don't know what to say, just keep repeating the prayer, "Lord, have mercy," or remain there in the silence.

3. Dedicate yourself and all your gifts, including your sexuality, to the Lord of Love.

4. Let the Lord's mercy flow over you like a gentle waterfall cleansing all guilt and shame: "Wash me, and I shall be whiter than snow" (Ps 51:7).

NOTES

1. Pope John Paul II, "Establishing the Ethical Sense," General Audience of October 1 and 8, 1980, in *The Theology of the Body*, 152–56.

2. Incidentally, I have never had an adult perpetrator confess sex with an underage person, but if that did happen, I would urge them to turn themselves in. Usually, I hear from the younger one being abused.

Chapter 9

Prayer

If prayer is a colloquy, a discussion, or a conversation of the
soul with God, then by prayer we speak to God and God in
turn speaks to us. We aspire to him and breathe in him; he
reciprocally inspires us and breathes upon us.

—St. Francis de Sales, *TLG*, 6:1

THE CONCEPT OF PRAYER

Young Timothy was at Grandma's house for dinner along with his Mom and Dad. When he immediately started digging into the food just set on the table, Mom said, "Wait, Timmy, we have to say grace." He was quick with a simple innocent answer, "We don't have to." Mom was a little perplexed, and asked, "Why would you say that, Tim? We always say grace at home." Tim looked at Mom and then at Dad and spoke innocently, "Well, that's at home; but we're at Grandma's now, and she *knows* how to cook."

So often our prayers and our concept of prayer are requests for perceived necessity. Young Tim thought it necessary to pray at home, but not at Grandma's because there was no need. We want this and we or somebody else needs that, and so we bring our requests to God, sometimes telling God exactly what he should do just in case God isn't clear about what to do. When what we wanted doesn't happen, we say that our prayers weren't answered. "Prayer doesn't work!" This concept seems so much less than what prayer means; like a newborn coming out of the womb, seeing the world, and feeling that it isn't a very interesting place. Or the child disappointed in not getting the Christmas gift he or she had requested from Santa Claus. Prayer is so much bigger than our needs, because God is so much bigger than our needs—and sometimes our perceived needs and wants are askew anyhow.

When my niece Jennifer was very little, she spotted the black olives on the table and started wanting one. We were sure she thought they were grapes, and we did everything to dissuade her from trying one. Finally, after her insistent requests, someone gave her an olive. Her contorted and disgusted face, followed by her spitting it out, made it clear that she really didn't know what she was asking for. Sometimes, it is like that with prayer.

An old definition for prayer is "lifting up our hearts and minds to God." Not too bad, except it gives the impression that prayer is something that *we* are doing, when in reality, *God* is the one who has opened the windows so that we might feel the breeze of the Spirit, and without God's willingness to do that, there would be nothing. Nevertheless, there certainly is a part we can play in praying, even though it is a response to God's grace.

Imagine prayer in the broadest possible relational experiences: for example, good friends visiting over lunch, taking a walk in the park or a ride in the country, seeing a movie, going fishing, sitting and watching TV, going to a presentation together, and so on. We could talk, laugh, hug, cry, or sit in silence on a bench saying nothing but watching the stream, or just hold each other. If we were wedded lovers, we could enter fully into a sexual union, the kind of union that brings new life. I think it is most helpful to think of prayer in the context of a *relationship* with God—being with God, whatever is going on.

You might say, "But God is *always* present, isn't he?" Precisely! God is present like the radio waves and phone signals that surround us, but aren't detectable until something is tuned into the frequency. Prayer is tuning into the frequency of God's permeating presence, paying attention, being aware of and mindful of God's presence; and there are millions of ways to do that! There are many prayers written, and many books on techniques of prayer from rhythmic mantras like the rosary to silent meditation. So, if you don't yet know how to pray, you can start reading, but more importantly you can start by praying. Like learning to ride a bike, before long you just have to do it.

THE PURPOSE OF PRAYER

Why would anyone even *want* to pray? I find it sad when people confess missing their prayers or even missing Mass on Sundays. Some people seem to feel the need to confess missing their prayers in order to keep God happy. They imply that God is perhaps angry with them because they didn't spend the "required" amount of time in prayer. Does God really care whether we pray at all? In Exodus, God does say, in what we call one of the commandments, "Remember the sabbath day, and keep it holy" (Exod 20:8). However, most of what follows is about not working, and instead resting, on the Sabbath of the Lord.

God wants us to pray, but not because he is a mean ogre who wants or needs his due attention or else he gets in a snit. God wants us to pray like a mother and father want their child to eat in order to be healthy enough to grow strong and build up immunity. Hear the Italian grandmother who says, "*Mange, mange!* You're all skin and bones! *Mange* (eat up)!" She wants you to eat up, to grow, to be strong. Think of prayer as food, or perhaps as energy. You want to be strong and resilient during the hardest times. Prayer is being aware of God's presence and love, and plugging into the very source of your life's power source.

Prayer is the nutrition, the energy, and the force that enable us to keep on trucking on this highway to heaven. It enables us to love and love some more, becoming more like Jesus, who is the visible revelation of the invisible God. Prayer is the transforming power of God, which isn't aimed at changing the Divine mind about something, but instead changing us personally or someone we are praying for. When we pray for something or for someone, we are lifting ourselves or them up in love, recommending them to God, and expressing our willingness to be instruments of God's love, doing whatever it is we can—from focusing our love on them to rolling up our sleeves and doing something practical. To pray for someone is not to wipe our hands of them and let God be responsible. There's a difference between loving someone and repeatedly lifting them up to God, and just saying, "I will pray for you" and forgetting about them.

Three women friends of Delores visited her at home where she was recovering from her illness. Toward the end of the visit, the women promised to pray for her. "Thank you very much," Delores responded, "I need all the help I can get, but while you're praying for me, would you be so kind as to do the dishes in the kitchen sink for me?"

When we pray for someone who is ill, we are praying that our love will support and help them; that they will be open to God's love, which is healing and encouraging; that the doctors and treatments will bring about the best results. Sometimes there is not only spiritual healing but dramatic physical healing, which can be declared miraculous. Who knows why some are healed and others are not? Do we assume that every prayer should be answered and that we all should keep living on this planet indefinitely?

BECOMING MINDFUL OF GOD

If God is omnipresent, or present everywhere, then we have the opportunity to become more mindful of that presence, as instructed by St. Paul: "Devote yourselves to prayer, keeping alert in it with thanksgiving" (Col 4:2).

Once we are attuned to God's presence, we don't want to lose consciousness of the great love that radiates from God. We want to become more mindful of God's presence throughout our day. This attentiveness doesn't happen simply by wishing it or even by making a resolution to be more attentive. It is a gift from above and the result of mindfulness training. Our brains can be shaped and literally changed by the thoughts and repeated behaviors that become part of our daily ritual. What we think about and what we do over and over again shape our brains and our worldview in dramatic ways. If we apply some of that insight to prayer and the mindfulness of God's presence, can we make ourselves more aware of God's presence?

The thoughts and directives of St. Francis de Sales and St. Jane de Chantal, in what was originally called the *Spiritual Directory*, is a proven method of mindfulness training. It has been practiced for the last four centuries by the Visitation of Holy Mary Sisters founded by St. Francis de Sales and St. Jane de Chantal, by the Oblates of St. Francis de Sales, the Lay Association of St. Francis de Sales, and others who have wanted to be more aware of God's presence.

A SPIRITUAL DIRECTORY
I. Life Direction

To set the foundation for all that follows, it is necessary to dedicate your entire life to the Lord; that is, to *direct the intention* of your entire life. Make God the declared intention and direction of your journey, so that even when you get off course, you'll know what direction to come back to. "I am yours, O God, and you are mine, and it will always be." Making such a devoted orientation a part of our lives needs to be firmly based in prayerful reflection and free decision. Write it down, look at it daily, and determine what you will do each day to move toward that dedication, that goal, that intention. The entire first section of De Sales's *Introduction to the Devout Life* is about making that intention firm. Even if you're not ready for the fullness of that commitment, you can still benefit from what follows, but it will be less effective, not as focused with only intermittent results. For example:

- Your destination point won't be as clear as doing everything for God's love;

- The directions on how to get there will keep changing since you don't quite know where the destination is; and

- Your mindfulness will be filled with incessant wanderings.

Imagine that you want to be filled with God and immersed in God, but your human heart is wounded and leaks like a sieve. You stand on the shore of the ocean of God's love and you try to scoop one handful at a time of the water of God's love into your heart, which does get wet, but immediately drains. There is only one way to fill that heart forever, and that is to toss it as far out onto the sea of God's love as you can. It will float for a bit, but then it will sink, and always be completely full to overflowing and immersed in God's love. That's the difference between making the full commitment and dedication to God and just dipping into devotion and spirituality. Which will it be for you?

II. Making the Life Direction a Habit

Once the life direction is made, it needs to be reinforced and deeply rooted in the psyche, so that it can become a habitual intention, a daily direction of intention, a renewing, a reminding, even an hourly orientation of everything we do, whether difficult or delightful. The best direction of intention is what comes from your own heart, in as few words as possible, and which can be memorized and repeated mentally or vocally in a few seconds. Here are some ideas that can be included in a regular mental direction of intention:

1. My God, you are here.

2. Help me love you right now.

3. All that I do, difficult or delightful, is for love of you.

4. Help me follow you by taking up my cross and carrying it as best I can.

Perhaps you can compose a direction of intention for yourself. In this day of short abbreviations and messages, my preference has become "All 4 U Lord." Decide what words you will use in your direction of intention, and rewrite them until you get what you like, and is really your own expression. Once you decide what those words are, you may want to make several copies to place around you so that you can eventually memorize them. For a whole month, you will read or say these words numerous times a day: when you get up, when you shower, when you eat, when you work, when you are walking, when you are ready to go to sleep, and literally anytime you can think of them. At least once a day, read the words aloud so as to form a habitual script in your brain. It takes about thirty days to create a neural pathway that can be permanent. You may even sing the words in whatever melody you choose. In the first month, you may forget to do it even for several days in a row. So it may take some time before it becomes a regular mental habit. Do not try to move onto the next step until you have perfected this one, since this step completes the foundation, and without much of a foundation, no building can stand for long.

III. Preparation of the Day

After getting that direction of intention to be as persistent as the GPS that tells you which way to go next, you're ready for some daily practice and growth. Spiritual growth sometimes happens in very dramatic events. We recall St. Paul being knocked down on the road to Damascus and experiencing the Risen Jesus in a moment of ecstasy (Acts 9), and we see what happens to some people after a near-death experience. However, for most of us, spiritual growth happens a step at a time, a day at a time, an hour at a time.

Following the foundational direction of intention is the morning exercise to prepare for the day ahead.

Morning prayer. If you don't already have one, write a morning prayer that expresses your intention for the day. You can add an Our Father, Hail Mary, and Glory Be.

Foresight. As you wake up, bring to mind the day of the week, the date, and what you have on your agenda for this day: school, work, a stressful commute, a day off, and the challenges that may predictably present themselves.

Plan of Action. As you bring to mind the day ahead and the realities that are to be faced, consider how you will deal with them: with strength, gentleness, kindness, charity, humor. For example, what will you say to the person at work who is always negative about everything and everybody? What can you say that might change the tone of the conversation without resentment? How about your own stress levels and impatience? How can you keep the day in balance?

Resolution. Here you firm up your direction of intention, resolving to do all the things you'll be doing for the love of God. You've decided to do it, you have a plan, and are now resolved to try it for today.

Recommendation. Now turn everything over to the Lord. "Come Holy Spirit, fill me, and help me do what I have just planned. I put myself into your hands in everything today."

Practice this Preparation of the Day for a month to make a habit of it before you move onto the next application.

IV. Hourly Applications

Having committed to your Direction of Intention and giving daily expression to your Direction of Intention, starting with your preparation of the day, you are now ready to complete the mindfulness training, spending a month training yourself in each of the following activities. Many of these activities you may do every single day. For example: breathe, wake, eat, drink, wash, get dressed, work, relax, travel, sleep, and more. Take each of these ten activities and craft a thought or prayer associated directly with the action. Here are some suggestions that associate a particular activity with an expression of religious thought. You can compose other prayers for these same activities and express religious thoughts for any number of other activities as you choose:

Breathing: Periodically, when you're a little too anxious or wound up, stop and pay attention to your breath. You may pray this or some other thought that you have composed: "Breathe into me your breath of life, O God, and make me fully alive" (*based on Gen 2:7*).

Waking: Waking up is like coming to life after being dead. You might pray: "You will raise me up this day and forever to new life, Lord Jesus" (*based on John 6:54*).

Eating: Anytime you have something to eat, you might pray this or other thoughts that you have composed: "O God, please nourish my heart and soul as this food does my body" (*based on John 6:55–58*).

Drinking: Whenever you drink something, you might pray this or some other thought that you compose: "Lord Jesus, give me that water that will spring up to eternal life" (*based on John 4:14*).

Washing: Whenever you wash your hands, take a shower, or even do laundry, you might pray this or another thought that you have composed: "Wash me, O Lord, and I shall be clean" (*based on Ps 51:7*).

Dressing: While you are dressing or changing clothes, you might pray this or other thoughts that you have composed: "Clothe me now with what I need for today's loving, O Lord" (*based on Col 3:12–14*).

Working: Depending on the kind of work you are doing, several possibilities come to mind. You might pray this or other thoughts that you have composed: "May the good work you have begun in me, Lord Jesus, be perfected" (*based on Phil 1:6*).

Relaxing: When it is time to relax, you might thank God for such Sabbath time and pray these or other thoughts that you have composed: "Let me taste of the fruit of your Spirit, O Lord, in joy, love, and peace" (*based on Gal 5:22*).

Traveling: Whether in a car, a plane, or a train, you might pray this or other thoughts: "Keep us safe by your presence within us, O Lord" (*based on Ezra 8:21*).

Retiring: When you are ready to go to bed, you'll want an intimate night prayer to be aware of God's great love for you. It is helpful to recall that the ultimate love of your life is God, who loves you all during the day and throughout the night, looking upon you like a parent looks on a sleeping child with delight. You can ask that the angels come and work on you during the night when there might be less resistance to becoming more like Jesus.

These conversational prayers to the Lord throughout the day are extremely helpful for the spiritual life. They are, perhaps, a natural outgrowth of it, and an unfailing support for the direction in life we are choosing.

MEDITATION

Many people have discovered that a time of silence, reading, and meditation is exceptionally beneficial not only for strengthening one's prayer life, but also for mellowing our days with a peaceful joy, even lowering our blood pressure! Furthermore, the more we meditate and focus on what is really important to us—on what we really want—those other things that bother us and tend to draw us away from what we deeply desire seem to fade away without even too much of a fight. Many of us have fought for years with various temptations and habits that we recognize are not good. However, we can't seem to help ourselves. Although all kinds of self-help programs can be beneficial, even inspired, such as the Twelve Steps of Alcoholics Anonymous, we will stop nonproductive behaviors and habits when we deeply desire something else more. Meditation helps me to see and desire that something else—contact with the divine presence in continual awareness and consciousness. Furthermore, I do not want a moment of the pain that being out of touch with that Divine Lover brings.

As a child, it seems so pious to pray oneself out of temptation. Why pray? Why would I miss the opportunity? I'd be a fool to do so. I want to be myself, and the best version of myself that I can be. Prayer is the power for growth in the Spirit.

Make frequent aspirations to God, by short but ardent movements of your heart; admire His beauty; implore His assistance; cast yourself in spirit at the foot of the Cross; adore His goodness; converse with him frequently; present your soul to him a thousand times a day; fix your interior eyes upon his sweetness; stretch out your hand to him, as a little child to his father, that he may lead you; place him in your heart, like a fragrant bouquet; plant him in your soul like a standard; and make a thousand different motions of your heart, to give you a love of God and to arouse yourself to a passionate and tender affection for this divine Spouse. (St. Francis de Sales, *IDL* 2:13)

DISTRACTIONS

After my first bout of cancer, Mom vowed to say the rosary every day for the rest of her life. I don't know whether she said the rosary specifically for me, or it was a bargained thanksgiving promise to God if I survived. One time, she complained to me about distractions while she was saying the rosary. We laughed and then I explained that our brains seldom travel a straight train-track path through the flatlands of the great plains. Rather, our brains operate more like a fistful of steel wool, with thoughts going every which way in a ball. This is normal, and so-called distractions are simply the way our creative brain works. So relax, distractions are normal. Think of your prayer time as focusing on the center of a daisy, time with and for God alone. No sooner do you start and the brain sends a different thought or distraction to the outer edge of one of the petals of the daisy. When you realize what's happened, catch that thought, turn it gently back into the center of the daisy, creating one of the flower's petals, and make it part of the prayer time. Of course, as soon as you do that, another thought will head out of the center and you'll need to catch it too and bring it back as another petal on the daisy. Your entire prayer time might be drawing daisies with the center focus being time with God. Do you still call those petals distractions?

Another approach is to imagine two good friends taking a walk in the park. It is a pleasant time to catch up with each other as well as get some exercise and fresh air. They update each other on their lives since they were last together and enjoy wherever the conversation takes them. Along the trail, they stop to check out some of the tiny flowers blooming on either side of the trail. They notice the sun's rays streaking through the trees, highlighting speckles of light and shades of green. They stop when they see a few deer, which also notice them. There is a boardwalk beside a stream and the bench there looks attractive enough that they sit in silence to watch and listen to the water, hunting for a glimpse of a fish or frog. Soon, they have circled back on the trail to their starting point. It was a delightful time together. Would either one of them say that they were "distracted" by the flowers, the sun, the deer, and the stream? It was part of the experience of being together, wasn't it? That's the way it can be with prayer. So let go of distractions, and include wherever your fertile mind goes into the experience of the walk in the park. It is largely a matter of reinterpretation.

SCRIPTURE REFLECTION

Once, when he was in one of the cities, there was a man covered with leprosy. When he saw Jesus, he bowed with his face to the ground and begged him, "Lord, if you choose, you can make me clean." Then Jesus stretched out his hand, touched him, and said, "I do choose. Be made clean." Immediately the leprosy left him. And he ordered him to tell no one. "Go," he said, "and show yourself to the priest, and, as Moses commanded, make an offering for your cleansing, for a testimony to them." But now more than ever the word about Jesus spread abroad; many crowds would gather to hear him and to be cured of their diseases. But he would withdraw to deserted places and pray. (Luke 5:12–17)

QUESTIONS FOR REFLECTION

1. Do I enter prayer with any expectations?

2. Can I pray anywhere, in any circumstance?

3. How much time would I make for meditation?

4. What place does prayer have in my life?

SUGGESTED ACTIVITIES

1. Develop your own Spiritual Directory as a means of mindfulness of God's presence.

2. Learn to meditate using the help of modern brain technology. Search the web for "meditation and brain technology." Combine it with your scriptural and devotional life.

3. If not the Bible, choose a small spiritual book to read and reflect on each day.

Chapter 10

Consolation and Hope

At the birth of our Lord Jesus Christ, the shepherds heard the angelic and divine hymns of those heavenly spirits—Scripture says so. Yet it is not said that Our Lady and St. Joseph, who were the closest to the child, heard the voice of the angels, or saw that miraculous light. On the contrary, instead of hearing these angels sing, they heard the child weep, and saw, by a little light borrowed from some wretched lamp, the eyes of this divine child all filled with tears, and faint under the rigor of the cold....I ask you in truth, would you not have chosen to be in the stable, dark and filled with the cries of the little baby, rather than to be with the shepherds, thrilling with joy and delight in this heavenly music and the beauty of this admirable light?

—Letter of St. Francis de Sales to Jane de Chantal,
August 6, 1606, *LST*, 145

SOLIDARITY

I first understood the meaning of solidarity when a young rookie New York City cop was killed in an off-duty car accident in Queens, New York. The funeral was to be at the small parish where I was doing a Mission. His wife was due to give birth to their first child on the day of the funeral. At that time there were about forty thousand New York City cops. Hardly any of them would know this young man. He was not killed on duty; no heroic performance making them all proud. However, he was one of theirs. The church was jammed, with loudspeakers on the outside

101

for the crowd that couldn't get in. Helicopters came in formation overhead, followed by a fleet of motorcycles leading the limousine and the hearse. Out stepped the pregnant, grieving wife. What I saw that day was solidarity—standing together, oneness, unity, not dependent on knowing or liking each other.

My sixth grade teacher at St. Francis de Sales Grade School in Toledo, Ohio, in 1957 was Sister Mary Cassilda, OSF, of the Joliet, Illinois, Franciscans. At the time, we thought that she was one year younger than God, although she was still alive almost twenty years later when I was ordained a priest. She was demanding and hot-tempered, and, while I complained to my mother about her every night, I got the best grades ever. There were a few Sisters in my grade school years with whom I fell in love, but Sister Cassilda was definitely not one of them. Nevertheless, I thank Sister Cassilda for introducing me to a devotion to the Sacred Heart of Jesus, which has been incredibly influential in my life and my vocation to the priesthood.

Grade school was a difficult period in my life. My father died of leukemia right after I started the first grade. Celebrating my First Holy Communion gave me the first real consolation as I began to develop a personal relationship with Jesus. At home there was a good guy who was my stepfather, but we were all dealing with his demons as an abused and abusive alcoholic. Unpredictable tensions and sometimes violent incidents were the norm. I hated it, so I tried to love school even more. Then there was the Sacred Heart of Jesus, the God-Man who loved me when my father and stepfather couldn't.

> Come to me, all you that are weary and are carrying heavy burdens, and I will give you rest. Take my yoke upon you, and learn from me; for I am gentle and humble in heart, and you will find rest for your souls. For my yoke is easy, and my burden is light. (Matt 11:28–30)

I recall staring at the picture of the Sacred Heart of Jesus with his heart surrounded by thorns and on fire with love and passion—for us, for me. I could relate to the pain, to the passion, and to the love that I craved.

Here was this God-Man who wanted my love and wanted me to let him love me. He became my refuge, my strength, through the next years of inner and outer conflict that characterized my junior and high school years. I had this secret place to go when I needed warmth, assurance, acceptance, forgiveness, and strength. It wasn't that he miraculously changed everything in the universe, but somehow I knew that I could survive with his help. Life was hard. I never expected things to come easily. Actually, I *expected* them to be hard, challenging but worth the struggle, because Jesus, my God, was with me.

The summer just before my father died, he took me out onto the back stoop during a thunderstorm, the kind we get around the Great Lakes region at that time of year. He crouched down in the baseball catcher's position and stood me in front of him—my pint-sized self between his legs—with his arms around me, and his head resting on my shoulder, so that he could talk directly into my right ear. As we listened to the storm and watched the lightning, he said, "Don't be afraid, Johnny, don't be afraid....Don't go and stand under a tree, since it could be knocked down and you could get hurt, but don't be afraid." That advice has been a sustaining image throughout my life—my Father with his strength surrounding me and his voice in my ear saying, "Do not be afraid."

Jesus became one of us, not just sharing in the beautiful and joyful moments—weddings, love, and family—but also taking on the difficulties and the suffering—poverty, refugees, social rejection, mockery, and even death. He wanted to come to us exactly where we were—in the mess that we were in. He would walk right with us in solidarity through the suffering of our lives.

Jesus companions us through the door of death to the kingdom of heaven. He would take us by the hand and lead us, or carry us, if we were collapsing in exhaustion. He is with us; he is with me. That's my consolation. It doesn't give meaning to my pain or answer the question why, it simply creates a perspective and reason to endure; a deep mysterious joy, which is quizzical to anyone without the same understanding. "Do not be afraid. I am right here beside you and around you."

THE PROBLEM OF EVIL

Recently I received an early morning text from my good friend Jim, who had called 911 after a deer was hit out in front of his house. Both its hind legs were broken, and it struggled in pain but could not stand up. Jim wrote, "There lies our human family, in pain and doing everything to try to stand up! Why?" Such an image. Such an insight. Such compassion!

Even since World War II, with the unbelievable atrocities and genocides of Hitler and the Nazis as well as the atomic bombings of Hiroshima and Nagasaki, the human species' capacity for homicidal evil seems commensurate with increased technology: China and Tibet (1950–69), North Korea (1948–94), Biafra (1967–70), Ethiopia(1975–78), Afghanistan (1979–82), Cambodia (1975–79), the former Yugoslavia (1992–99), Rwanda (1994), the Sudan, and 9/11 in the United States, to name just a few of the better known.

When we ask why bad things happen to good people, we shouldn't focus exclusively on ourselves. Of course, the questions are much larger. Why do we experience such evil? There are many attempted answers, but none is totally comprehensible.

At times, I don't understand my own attraction to evil, let alone that of the rest of humanity. How do we process some of the awful things that we have done or that have happened to us personally and to others whom we love, not to mention the rest of humanity? How do we maintain any optimism or hope given even our own participation in the unbelievable sin of the world? Our inky footprints are found everywhere.

While our personal spirituality can speak of beauty, consolation, and communion with the Divine, we also have to deal with the bloody murder of the Son of God on the cross—not only in his life, but also in our own. Jesus did not use his power as God to escape from the evil that exists in the world. He went directly into it, walking right through the hell of evil to its deadly conclusion, so that every bit of human life and context might be transformed by hope.

Certainly, hope can't possibly be based on what we see of the current situation of this world, which, at times, is pitiful. However, we cannot despair on the one hand or blithely accept everything, passively waiting on God to do something, on the other. We have to be courageous and let go of despair in the present, and be committed to a future—our future—doing whatever we can to make a difference. Here is the place for brave optimism. Not the glass-is-half-full variety. But a courageous optimism of hope that works on a vision of the future well beyond what we are experiencing now, even when we don't understand quite why or how anything around us is unfolding the way it is. We can hope because we know that the loving God is with us, walking with us, and leading us to the kingdom.

God does not make us suffer. There is randomness to the created universe, which has the maximum discretion of its own freedom within which to operate, including galaxies and stars; microbes and electrons; lions, tigers, and bears, as well as humans. God doesn't determine who will get cancer or be killed in a car accident, or who will be born with severe mental disabilities or die today. Rather, God equips his beloved children with the grace and power to deal with the challenges of his created universe in an ongoing creative and mysterious way.

Furthermore, I don't see that it is helpful to accept such crosses like some distasteful medicine or painful therapy because

God, the Divine and Loving Physician, gives it to us for the purpose of our healing or ultimate good. That has worked for many saints, but I find it odd. Perhaps it helps as a coping mechanism. The Awesome Lover, whom I have come to know, simply doesn't design painful training exercises with obstacle courses so that I get tougher and more capable. The way I see it, God has no need to design such training programs, since the randomness of the universe already provides plenty of challenges. What God does is pour out incredible grace that gives hope, endurance, and persistence to inventively create personal and social methods and structures for the betterment of reality. God has already poured out that grace in giving us our share in his creative power, but he continues his presence, saturation, and immersion in existence. While I don't claim to understand God's designs or the working of the universe, can we at least begin to think about these problems in a new way, since evil is so massive and screams for a new way of understanding God's Providence?

God continues to give creation as much power and freedom as he gave it in the first place. This power and freedom includes the death of stars; the moving of tectonic plates on earth, resulting in earthquakes and tsunamis; typhoons and hurricanes; viruses and bacteria; tumors and traveling cells that spread the cancers; Ponzi schemes; abuse and the denigration and mistreatment of life forms. God is more committed to freedom than any American idealist ever thought possible, because love, which can never be forced, depends on freedom, not just of conscious humans, but (can we say) of all creation.

> When our divine Savior is near death...with a loud cry and many tears he says, "Alas, O my Father, into your hands I commend my spirit." This was last of all his words, and by it the beloved son gave supreme testimony to his love for his Father. Therefore, when all things fail us, when our distress is at its height, this

word, this sentiment, this renouncement of our soul
into the hands of our Savior cannot fail us. When con-
vulsive spiritual torments deprive us of every other
kind of relief and means of resistance, let us commend
our spirit into the hands of the eternal Son, who is our
true Father, and "bowing the head," of our acquies-
cence in his good pleasure, let us consign our entire
will to him. (St. Francis de Sales, *TLG*, 9:12)

THE DIVINE LOVER

So what is a person to do? Refuse to quit. Do not throw
down your tools and go home. Do not take your ball and refuse to
play. Never give up on yourself, on others, or on the whole world.
Never lose your courage. Never dismiss your courage; that is
called *dis*couragement. Do the best you can. Make the change you
want to see in the world in yourself. Use the creative power of your
mind, spirit, and body, and stand together to work with others to
do whatever you can. Do everything possible and even try some
things that everyone else thinks are impossible. From moment to
moment, do the next loving thing. Ask the Spirit for the strength
and creativity to know what the next loving thing is. Take up your
cross and follow Jesus one step at a time, entering into solidarity
and suffering with every part of groaning creation, knowing that
God accompanies us and leads us beyond what we thought was
ever possible. That's the tradition of uniting with the suffering
Jesus and, in solidarity, also with his offering.

Some prayer images from St. Francis de Sales are helpful in
the most painful moments, for they make us aware of the reality
that God is here. In difficult times, my favorite image is the base
of the cross, which is like the mast of the ship (of life), rocking and
rolling on the stormy seas. All you have to do is hang on. There is
no need to say or pray anything. Another image is that of Jesus at

the Last Supper with the beloved disciple. Feel his heart beat and see if you can get your heart to beat together with his. Again, nothing needs to be said.

There are so many images from the Gospels that can help us focus on Jesus, not only through times of consolation, but also to give us the strength to endure the crosses that we are carrying. Indeed, it is the Divine Lover who is the object of our love, not the consolation. Welcome consolation when it comes and for as long as it lasts. In my vulnerability, in my weakness, and even in my sin, I have needed those encouragements in order to hang on, to remember that I am loved incredibly because God is such an awesome lover, and to keep trying to be the best me, the best lover that I am capable of being with the help of God's Spirit.

SCRIPTURE REFLECTION

Six days later, Jesus took with him Peter and James and John, and led them up a high mountain apart, by themselves. And he was transfigured before them, and his clothes became dazzling white, such as no one on earth could bleach them. And there appeared to them Elijah with Moses, who were talking with Jesus. Then Peter said to Jesus, "Rabbi, it is good for us to be here; let us make three dwellings, one for you, one for Moses, and one for Elijah." He did not know what to say, for they were terrified. Then a cloud overshadowed them, and from the cloud there came a voice, "This is my Son, the Beloved; listen to him!" Suddenly when they looked around, they saw no one with them any more, but only Jesus. As they were coming down the mountain, he ordered them to tell no one about what they had seen, until after the Son of Man had risen from the dead. So they kept the matter to themselves, questioning what this rising from the dead could mean. (Mark 9:2–10)

QUESTIONS FOR REFLECTION

1. How aware am I of the depth of evil in our history?

2. How do I cope when bad things happen?

3. What fortifies my faith and gives me hope?

4. In this chapter, what are the points with which I agree and disagree?

SUGGESTED ACTIVITIES

1. Start an ongoing list of joys and consolations in your life, small and large.

2. Start an ongoing list of what you have considered the crosses in your life.

3. Share these joys and crosses with someone you trust.

Chapter 11

Spirituality of the Present Moment

Come now, keep your eyes lifted up on high to God; increase your holy humility, fortify it with meekness, confirm it by a steady effort; always make your mind rule over your inclinations and moods, do not allow fears to take hold of your heart; the effort you make one day will teach you what to do the next day. You have before now conquered many a difficulty, and you did it by God's grace; the same grace will be with you on future occasions and will deliver you from difficulties and rough roads as you come upon them, for God will send an angel to carry you over the most dangerous places.

—St. Francis de Sales, *LST*, 234

A teacher can usually tell if someone in the class is not really present. Their mind is elsewhere, perhaps on some exciting adventure, or caught in anxiety about what's going on at home. Their eyes may be glazed over.

One would think that being in the present is the easiest thing in the world. However, we are often spending time with past memories or anticipating future delights, or perhaps anxieties, from the sublime (Am I going to heaven or hell?) to the silly (I hope this pimple on my nose disappears before the wedding next week).

THE PRESENT MOMENT

St. Francis de Sales wrote to many people about their anxieties over the past and future, always recommending that they try to remain in the present and let go of the concerns of the past or the future. His teaching is indeed a spirituality of the present moment. Francis came to this place in his own life after a number of events helped him understand the wisdom of the present moment.

In 1584, at the age of seventeen, the young Francis would sit in on theology lectures at the Sorbonne in Paris. In particular, one lecture series on the Song of Songs from the Hebrew Scriptures by the French Benedictine scripture scholar, Gilbert Génébrard, captivated him. The lectures explored the poetic nature of the pursuing love of a bride and groom as the love affair between God and his people, between God and the individual soul. God, the groom, is the Divine Lover in a love ballet with his bride. Already in love with God, this image held great appeal for Francis de Sales, so much so that he adopted it as the primary image of God for the rest of his life.

Later, in 1586, at the age of nineteen and still a student in Paris, Francis was experiencing many temptations so attractive that he wondered whether he was destined for hell. Furthermore, it was at a time when John Calvin was presenting the notion of predestination *apart* from an individual's choice or effort. This thought created an intense crisis and conflict for Francis— although deeply in love with the Divine Lover, he could possibly be destined for hell! His anxiety kept him awake at nights and he wasn't eating well. In fact, his friends began to worry that, if he was going to hell, it would be damn soon. In his inner torment, one day on his way home from school, he stopped at the church of Sainte Etienne de Gras (St. Stephen of the Fields) to pray in the side chapel of the Black Madonna.[1]

It was here at prayer that it occurred to him that although he didn't know whether he would be able to love God for eternity, he could at least love him now, in this present moment. As a result, he effectively let go of the anxiety about his future eternity in heaven. He abandoned himself to God's mercy and decided not to worry about loving God in a future that was not yet here, but to love God now in a present that was here. Furthermore, he would continue to do this in the every "now" of his life. Concluding this prayer experience, Francis prayed the *Memorare*, which he found on a card nearby:

> Remember, O Most Gracious Virgin Mary,
> that never was it known,
> that anyone who fled to thy protection,
> implored thy help, or sought thy intercession was left
>   unaided.
> Inspired by this confidence, I fly onto thee,
> O Virgin of virgins, My Mother.
> To thee I come, before thee I stand, sinful and
>   sorrowful.
> O Mother of the Word Incarnate,
> despise not my petitions,
> but in thy mercy, hear and answer me. Amen.

Years later, Francis would write to Jane de Chantal stating that following this prayer experience, it was as if scales fell from his eyes and his anxieties left him. It was the birth of what came to be known as his spirituality of the present moment. Who knows what you will be able to do in the future. What can you do *now* to heal and repair the past or to build on in the future?

REMEMBERING THE PAST

At Sacred Heart Church in Covina, California, there was an older widow and a widower who grew very fond of each other.

They wondered whether they should consider marrying each other. She wondered whether she could stand to clean up for yet another man. He speculated as to whether he could live with another woman that knew just the right way that everything should be done. He was the bashful type, and it was going to take some gumption to ask her to marry him, but one day he did it. She smiled and said something, but he didn't quite catch it. Judging from her smile, he thought she had said "yes," but wasn't sure. He didn't want to ask her to repeat herself, because then she might think he was a little deaf, which, of course, he was. So he just smiled and tried to replay the conversation hoping it would become clearer, but it didn't. At home that night nothing became any clearer to him, so he decided that he really simply needed to call her first thing in the morning and tell her the situation. She was so understanding; that's one of the things he really liked about her. She said, "Oh, I said 'yes' and I really meant it. I am so glad that you called though, since I forgot who had asked."

There is a difference between remembering the past and living in it. You don't want to live in the past—the adventures, events, victories, glories, and loves—in such a way that you miss what's going on right now. Memory is the incredible gift of spending time in the past, *remembering great sights, experiences, and people* in our lives, and *being delighted again by recalling and reliving the feelings.* Celebrations such as birthdays and anniversaries do this. We can do it in prayer as well.

Facing Our Reality

Living the *pain and suffering of the past* can be more challenging. It is important to see those difficult realities in a different light and from a distance, until we are free from their devastating grip on us, and can be thankful that we got through them, and learned a few things in the process.

The past may bring anxieties, guilt, and shame, or resentments and anger, as a result of hurtful memories and tragic consequences. How do you deal with these memories and consequences?

Like the Twelve Steps of Alcoholics Anonymous, owning up to the exact nature of your past dysfunction and sins is healthy spiritual living. Steps four and five of the original Twelve Steps published by Alcoholics Anonymous ask the alcoholic to make a searching and fearless moral inventory and then to admit to God, to oneself, and to another human being the exact nature of the wrongs.

As a priest, I am privileged in the sacrament of Reconciliation to be present with a person in prayer; to be in role of the father of the prodigal son, in fact, in the role of Jesus himself: being there for someone struggling, wrestling with God and life, and hurting from their failures:

> But while he was still far off, his father saw him and was filled with compassion; he ran and put his arms around him and kissed him. Then the son said to him, "Father, I have sinned against heaven and before you; I am no longer worthy to be called your son." But the father said to his slaves, "Quickly, bring out a robe—the best one— and put it on him; put a ring on his finger and sandals on his feet. And get the fatted calf and kill it, and let us eat and celebrate; for this son of mine was dead and is alive again; he was lost and is found!" (Luke 15:20–24)

There is something incredibly therapeutic in owning up to and sharing the exact nature of our flaws and sins, and being accepted and loved for who we are and for who we are willing to become. It is facing our reality.

In 1980, after taking the MMPI (Minnesota Multiphasic Personality Inventory), the counselor was ready to share the feedback with me. He said that I had a tendency to whitewash myself. I gulped and asked, "What do you mean?" He said, "Let me give you one of several examples. The inventory asked if you tell lies, and you checked 'never.' Really? Never?" I insisted that that was correct. He asked again, "Really?...Never?" I had to admit that that probably couldn't be true. He pointed out that I was projecting my value of honesty, which was a good thing, though I really couldn't always live up to it perfectly. In presenting my ideal self—not the real self—I was whitewashing myself!

In facing my reality, I throw myself before God, the Awesome One, who loves me so much, and beg for mercy. God has been waiting for me to let go of my past, to accept healing of my shame, to know forgiveness of my sins. If there is a voice that insists on reminding us of our past sins, we can say in humility, "Yes, it is true. I have sinned and I still struggle. But Jesus died so that I would be forgiven and no longer need to be ashamed."

Clare Boothe Luce noted the response of St. Francis de Sales when confronted by the reality of forgiveness and mercy in a woman who came to him in confession:

> When one of the outstanding "grand prostitutes" of the day, summoning a desperate courage came to him, made her confession, and having made it collapsed in horror at the exposure of her true self, St. Francis rose from his seat of judgment and absolution. He raised the woman to her feet, himself knelt before her and, to fasten her grasp on God's granted grace, told her that he so knelt because he was now in the presence of a sinless soul.[2]

If you are still plagued by thoughts of your past, regularly place your wounded heart into the heart of the Lord Jesus and pray for healing. This isn't so much a one-time event as much as a life habit. You may even need the help of a counselor to help you let go of a past that is no doubt preventing you from growing spiritually in the present.

DO NOT BE AFRAID

How secure is the future? Financially, the world economy could collapse. A simple bank foreclosure or tornado could change our home life. An errant driver could eliminate whatever health we or a loved one already have. We really don't have a lot of security promised during our time on the planet. Scripture tells us to look to the divine and heavenly promises with hope and faith:

> Then the Lord GOD will wipe away the tears from all faces, and the disgrace of his people he will take away from all the earth, for the LORD has spoken. (Isa 25:8)

> Then in my flesh I shall see God, whom I shall see on my side, and my eyes shall behold, and not another. (Job 19:26–27)

> Those who eat my flesh and drink my blood have eternal life, and I will raise them up on the last day. (John 6:54)

Security in *this* world is flimsy. God has a much longer and broader view of existence than this time-bound earthly creation. As Jesus said,

> They will put some of you to death. You will be hated by all because of my name. But not a hair of your head will perish. By your endurance you will gain your souls. (Luke 21:16–19)

The Eternal God has a different perspective on life and time from us. A man had a vision from God and hardly knew what to say. While stammering and stuttering, he asked, "God?...ah, what is a billion years like to you?" "Oh," God said, as he snapped his fingers, "a billion years is just barely a second." Still not knowing quite what he was saying, the man continued, "Then, what...what is a billion dollars like to you?" The Lord rolled his eyes and said, "Well, it is just barely a penny. Why do you ask, my child?" The man bowed his head and shuffled his feet a bit, before finally having enough courage to ask, "God, could I have, I mean...if it wouldn't be too much trouble...could I have one of your pennies?" God laughed, and said, "Sure, just a second," as he snapped his fingers. God sees differently from us.

Maybe it is because our security is so fragile on this planet that we find ourselves plagued with fears about everything imaginable. The Bible uses the word *fear* and *afraid* well over six hundred times, suggesting that it is a big part of our human psyche and something the Lord wishes to address. Here are a few examples:

> But now thus says the LORD, he who created you, O Jacob, he who formed you, O Israel: *Do not fear*, for I have redeemed you; I have called you by name, you are mine....Because you are precious in my sight, and honored, and I love you, I give people in return for you, nations in exchange for your life. *Do not fear*, for I am with you; I will bring your offspring from the east, and from the west I will gather you. (Isa 43:1–5)

> *Do not be afraid*, little flock, for it is your Father's good pleasure to give you the kingdom. (Luke 12:32)

> I tell you, my friends, *do not fear* those who kill the body, and after that can do nothing more. But I will warn you whom to fear: fear him who, after he has killed, has authority to cast into hell. Yes, I tell you,

fear him! Are not five sparrows sold for two pennies? Yet not one of them is forgotten in God's sight. But even the hairs of your head are all counted. *Do not be afraid*; you are of more value than many sparrows. (Luke 12:4–7)

Fear plays an important role in our lives. It might be fear that protects us from getting too close to the cliff. We may worry about a young child who doesn't yet have the sense to fear what could be seriously harmful and even deadly. However, while fear can be a protective mechanism, it can also paralyze us to such an extent that we are unable to respond or have the sense to flee from the danger. The opossum, for example, when threatened or harmed, will "play possum," mimicking the appearance and smell of a sick or dead animal and emitting a foul smell to make itself less attractive to prey. While such an action might work in avoiding a coyote, it is counterproductive in the middle of a highway, in the path of a car or truck.

Fear of the Lord also has its place, if understood correctly. The power of the Lord may inspire more awe than the Grand Canyon, an active volcano, or the Amazon jungle. We may even be instinctively wary before such power and might. However, when we come to know and experience the love of this Divine Lover, such fear can be tamed.

Planning for the Future

Fear of the future often presents itself as anxiety and worry. Spending time and energy worrying about what might happen can wear us down, and make us less able to deal with the difficulties when they occur. It is sometimes good to plan for what is possible. Having a fire drill at school or work is never a bad idea—knowing what to do if there was a fire, or planning what to do if a biopsy result was positive, are helpful.

Sometimes, it is good to consider how you might deal with the worst case scenario. Figuring out how you might handle that makes everything else much easier. Most importantly, trust in the Lord, no matter what, and always make the best out of every moment—*the present*—until the time for death arrives.

Nothing is more certain than the inevitability of death, yet we spend so much time denying it, considering it morbid to even discuss. Be prepared for what might happen, but don't waste energy on being anxious and worrying; these are not only useless, but even worse, they disable our energy to enjoy and respond to the moment—our response-ability—to events as they happen. Worry and anxiety are worth letting go so that we can experience the joy of this moment now.

While studying in Paris, Francis de Sales saw wisdom in letting go of anxiety about his future, even in going to heaven. He knew that he could affect the present and developed a spirituality based on dealing with reality as it is; doing the best he could in every moment, being as gentle and at peace as possible, always trusting in the Divine Lover, and asking Mother Mary for support.

> How soon we shall be in the realm of eternity! And then we shall see how little all the affairs of this world amount to and how little it mattered whether they did or did not succeed; but all the same, now we pursue them as though they were great things. When we were small, how eagerly we put together little bits of tiles and wood and mud to make houses and tiny buildings! And if someone smashed them, how very miserable we were and how we wept; but now we see how very unimportant it all was. One day we shall experience the same thing in heaven when we see that what we clung to in this world was nothing more than a child's fancy. (St. Francis de Sales, *LST*, 152)

SCRIPTURE REFLECTION

Therefore I tell you, do not worry about your life, what you will eat, or about your body, what you will wear. For life is more than food, and the body more than clothing. Consider the ravens: they neither sow nor reap, they have neither storehouse nor barn, and yet God feeds them. Of how much more value are you than the birds! And can any of you by worrying add a single hour to your span of life? If then you are not able to do so small a thing as that, why do you worry about the rest? Consider the lilies, how they grow: they neither toil nor spin; yet I tell you, even Solomon in all his glory was not clothed like one of these. But if God so clothes the grass of the field, which is alive today and tomorrow is thrown into the oven, how much more will he clothe you! (Luke 12:22–28)

QUESTIONS FOR REFLECTION

1. Are there any concerns about my past that continue to haunt me?

2. What choices do I have regarding my present life?

3. What are my anxieties and worries about the future?

4. How would I let go of any anxieties that I have at the moment?

SUGGESTED ACTIVITIES

1. Make a general confession of your whole life.

2. Make amends to people you may have hurt.

3. Enter a forgiveness process for those who have hurt you.

4. Talk to a counselor or spiritual director.

5. Write down what you would do this month if you knew it would be your last.

NOTES

1. The statue of Notre Dame de Bonne Délivrance is a fourteenth-century replica of an eleventh-century original, a Black Madonna and Child. The church building was destroyed in the French Revolution, but the statue was preserved by Madame de Carignon who, in 1806 when she was freed after having been arrested for her Catholicism in the Reign of Terror, gave the statue to the Sisters of St. Thomas of Villeneuve, who had been imprisoned with her. The statue is currently located in the Sisters' chapel in Neuilly-sur-Seine outside Paris.

2. Clare Boothe Luce, *Saints for Now* (New York: Sheed and Ward, 1952), 266.

Chapter 12
Holy Indifference

St. Ignatius of Loyola founded the Society of Jesus. He saw so many beautiful fruits. He foresaw many more in the future. Yet, he had the courage to resolve that even though he should see it all destroyed, which should be the bitterest disappointment he could experience, then with half an hour he would be unwaveringly calm in God's will.

—St. Francis de Sales, *TLG*, IX, 6

After a triple bypass surgery, I found myself depressed and wondering whether anything really mattered. Eventually, I decided that much of my depression was caused by the medication, and so I asked my doctor whether it was still needed. After changing my medication, my disposition also changed in a relatively short time.

HUMAN DESIRES

Holy indifference is neither depression nor some stoic discipline of maintaining composure, self-control, and coolness at all costs. Holy indifference is based on the simple willingness to adventurously cope with and respond to everything the universe presents to us, knowing that God is our help and companion to the end. It is a combination of hope and the ability to let go of our hopes and expectations and to allow whatever God wills.

Much of our suffering is the result of human desires that go unmet. We really want something—health, wealth, intimacy, or holiness—and we hurt when we don't get it. If we can reduce or elim-inate our desires, we can reduce or eliminate some of our suffering.

Desires can also motivate change in us and in the world, and are the making of dreams and visions. Consequently, rather than having no desires, we should be comfortable in letting go of cer-tain desires, or altering and transforming those desires into new ones that fit the reality of our life.

For example, when I left home at the age of eighteen to join the priesthood, my first year as a postulant and my second year as a novice went well as I embraced my vocation and Salesian spiritual-ity.[1] Following the year in the novitiate, I joined the community and began studying for a Bachelor of Science. At the beginning of my second semester, I was diagnosed with a parotid cancer in the right salivary gland. This was definitely not in the game plan. However, if I was going to play at all, I needed to get with the program quickly.

What about my desire to become a priest? Following the year in the novitiate, I was certain that nothing mattered as much as my relationship with the Lord. I had made a decision that I was going to be his and he would be mine. I would carry whatever my cross was and follow him. I recall praying after returning home the evening of that preliminary diagnosis, with surgery already sched-uled: "Lord, I said I will follow you and carry my cross, but I had no idea that my health would be my cross, and that it would be so soon! I'm not reneging. I still want to be with you and you to be with me, and I meant it. So what is this going to mean? Will I live? Will I die?…Lord, I'll be fine with whatever happens next. I am a little scared, but I am willing to die happy, or live happy, as long as I am with you."

A powerful image that has remained with me from that experience is the image of the mother nursing her infant at her breast. Whether the mother sits or stands, or is going east or west, doesn't matter to the infant. I am now that infant in God's arms. Of course, there was still the desire to become a priest, but through incredible grace, this desire had become flexible.

The day after the surgery, my head was wrapped in white, like the old habits that nuns used to wear, but without a veil, and the dressing was much larger on the right side. I was shocked to see that beneath the dressing, a large chunk had been removed from the side of my head and face. At that moment, dying looked heroic, but the living seemed humiliating. Soon, I was rejoicing more to be surviving and thriving than being depressed over my disfigurement.

Two years later a couple of amazing plastic surgeries would improve my looks enough to reduce my self-consciousness. However, what really mattered throughout this period of illness was my faith in God's presence, which allowed me to let go of my human desires and accept and respond to God's will as much as possible. Knowing that everything is embraced by a divine care and presence gave me peace.

God didn't give me cancer, although he did allow it to happen. Of course, how flexible would I have been in my desire to become a priest if my health prevented it?

Holy indifference does not mean not caring about what happens, rather, it's about making the best of whatever happens with equal joy because God is present. God, who is love, is present and loving in any situation because all reality is saturated, immersed in God. St. Jane de Chantal is inspiring regarding this topic when she writes to her sisters in community:

> We must seek God alone, wish for God alone, tend to God alone. Ah! If you only seek God, you will find him everywhere; for example: one of you is going to prayer, obedience takes her off immediately to employ her elsewhere; without fail, she will find God as much in this occupation as in her prayers. I grant you that perhaps it will be with less satisfaction and sweet repose. If you seek only God, Sisters, you will be indifferent about your employment, your tasks, your house and everything concerning you, inasmuch as you will find

everywhere the good and great God of your heart since he is never better found than in obedience. It is in this divine indifference that we find enclosed the teaching of our Blessed Father (Francis de Sales): Ask for nothing, refuse nothing. (*CJC*, 152)

Holy indifference is to desire whatever God allows to happen. It may not be easy, for it means letting go of our own human desires, and surely, we are creatures who want our own way and will. Perhaps this is what is meant when Jesus speaks of dying:

Very truly, I tell you, unless a grain of wheat falls into the earth and dies, it remains just a single grain; but if it dies, it bears much fruit. (John 12:24)

THE ABILITY TO LOVE

My aunt Joie called me from Florida during her last days. She asked me if heaven, the afterlife, and God were all for real. I laughed heartily as I had in many of our conversations. "Well, I certainly believe so. I've bet my whole life on it, so to speak. Personally, it's not about belief in heaven or the afterlife, but rather belief in the God of my life and experience.

"But you know what?" I continued, "I am not sure that the existence of heaven and the afterlife will really matter....I have tried to live by the law of love as much as I could, and it has been a *great* life....The values of Jesus and the Gospels are the best way and most joyful way to live without doubt...I really don't have many regrets, and if I did want to do anything differently, it would be to love more and better than I did. I have had heaps of love. I have loved many people who have also loved me. I have loved a great deal of nature and science, the arts, thought and knowledge, and the pleasures of being alive. If anything, I'd just like to be able to have loved more. I am going to die happy in the Lord's embrace. What on earth do I have to lose? All earthly pleasures, lusts, greed, and pride are so pitifully pale when compared with the heights and depth of love."

I surprised myself in sharing this lesson with Aunt Joie—to love the present moment regardless of the presence or not of an afterlife.

While in Louisiana doing a parish Mission, I went to visit a grandmother taking care of her handicapped granddaughter, Elizabeth. She was eighteen and in bed, diapered, and as small as a five-year-old child. She had never walked nor spoken. She had been thrown against the wall as an infant by one of her drug-addicted parents for crying just one too many times. Grandma had a heart condition and was concerned about what might happen to Elizabeth when she was gone. Was Elizabeth injured because she was less lovable than other infants? Certainly not! How much a person is loved depends on who is doing the loving. Loving is not determined by whether you are, or anyone else is, lovable. Unfortunately, Elizabeth's parents were unable to love, but the grandmother was. Love is never so dependent on the one being loved as the one who is doing the loving. God is infinitely capable of love, for God is Love. We must strive to become more like that Lover with every breath.

Learn to love loving; absorb as much of it as you can so that you can give as much as you can. Do the next loving thing. Rejoice in every moment, respond to the challenge of the universe, and hang onto everything good that you can, letting go of anything that impedes your ability to love.

SCRIPTURE REFLECTION

They went to a place called Gethsemane; and he said to his disciples, "Sit here while I pray." He took with him

Peter and James and John, and began to be distressed and agitated. And he said to them, "I am deeply grieved, even to death; remain here, and keep awake." And going a little farther, he threw himself on the ground and prayed that, if it were possible, the hour might pass from him. He said, "Abba, Father, for you all things are possible; remove this cup from me; yet, not what I want, but what you want. (Mark 14:32–36)

QUESTIONS FOR REFLECTION

1. Do I live my life only for the promise of heaven?

2. What really matters most to me?

3. Is whatever happens in the universe the same as God's permissive will?

4. What do I agree with and disagree with in this chapter?

SUGGESTED ACTIVITIES

1. Make a short list of your deepest desires. How do you react if they are not met?

2. Can you hang onto the Lord now, regardless of whether you can in the future?

3. Does hanging onto God depend on your religious beliefs?

NOTES

1. See Appendix III.

Appendix I

St. Francis (François) de Sales (1567–1622)

François Bonaventura de Sales was named after his father, François, his Mother, Françoise, and their patron, St. Francesco of Assisi. Francis of Assisi had been born four hundred years earlier, while the life of French-speaking de Sales overlapped with Galileo Galilei, William Shakespeare, Montaigne, Teresa of Avila, John of the Cross, Charles Borromeo, Robert Bellarmine, and Louis XIII of France. He regarded the Duchy of Savoy (today the Alpine region where France, Italy, and Switzerland meet) as his homeland.

Francis de Sales was educated in the Christian humanist tradition, mostly by the Jesuits in Paris and Padua, two of the largest and most prestigious centers of higher learning in Europe. He was a civil and a church lawyer, but his fondest interests led him to theology and the desire for the priesthood. As a young priest, he undertook a difficult and dangerous mission to preach the Catholic faith near Geneva, where he treated both Protestants and Catholics as brothers and sisters. Writing religious tracts, which he slipped under peoples' doors when they were afraid to come to listen to his gently persuasive and charismatic preaching in public, he succeeded in attracting thousands back to the Catholic faith.

As a reforming post–Council-of-Trent bishop, he focused on the education of the clergy and laity. His famous *Introduction to the Devout Life* of 1609, which began as letters of spiritual direction, spoke of people being holy, whether in the workshop, the court, the kitchen, or the convent. Today, he is one of only thirty-five Doctors of the Church whose teachings are regarded as valuable for every Christian. Pope Paul VI said that Francis de Sales anticipated the Second Vatican Council's universal call to holiness. He is patron of writers, the Catholic Press, and the hearing-impaired.

St. Jeanne-Françoise (Jane) Frémyot de Chantal (1572–1641)

In English, we know her as St. Jane de Chantal. Her father, Bénigne Frémyot, remarried after his wife's death in childbirth with Jane's younger brother André, but this second wife also died in childbirth, as did her child. Jane was the middle child between Marguerite and André, and without a mother, they were raised under the father's direction with the help of a paternal aunt and a good tutor. Being of noble Burgundian birth and living in the capital city of Dijon, she benefited from a good education and considerable social exposure. Her arranged marriage to Christophe de Rabutin, the second Baron de Chantal, worked out exceptionally well and the couple loved each other deeply. Their first two children died immediately after they were born, but there were four others who then survived. Right after the birth of her last child, Christophe was shot in a hunting accident and died some days later. Jane, with four little children at the age of twenty-nine, was devastated by her situation.

In 1604, Jane's brother and father encouraged her to come to the Lenten parish Mission to be encouraged and uplifted. The preacher was to be none other than the new bishop of Geneva, Francis de Sales. The relationship and correspondence of the people who would become these two great saints, has graced us with the best documented celibate Christian relationship of a man and woman. In 1610, they cofounded the Visitation of Holy Mary, a religious community of women very different for its time in terms of its gentle spirit and outreach to the poor. Jane became the Mother and energetic foundress of over eighty monasteries of Sisters before she died in 1641. After the death of Francis de Sales, her spiritual director was Vincent de Paul.

St. Jane is a wonderful patron for women today: she was educated, charming, and entertaining; a loving wife; a mother, who gave birth to six children; an efficient organizer and administrator, always with the gentleness of a mother's touch; a widow, who had difficult and depressing times dealing with her father-in-law; a religious founder; and a suffering mourner, who not only lost her mother, but ultimately her husband, five of her six children, as well as her closest friend, Francis de Sales.

Salesian Spirituality

WHAT IS SALESIAN SPIRITUALITY?

The word *Salesian* (Suh LEEZH ee an) refers to the name of the estate where St. Francis de *Sales* was born. It has come to mean the Christian humanist school of thought and expression that flowed from St. Francis de Sales and St. Jane de Chantal, and is preserved in Francis de Sales's collected writings (twenty-six volumes), and in the institutions that have grown out of that historical tradition.

First and foremost among these institutions would be the community of the Visitation of Holy Mary, which St. Jane de Chantal and Francis cofounded. The Visitation community not only tried to live the spirit of their founders, but to spread it as well. Numerous religious communities, diocesan associations, and lay groups in many countries have been influenced and have adopted the Salesian spirit and style over the last four centuries. One of those religious communities was founded by St. John Bosco and was called the Society of St. Francis de Sales until after the canonization of St. John Bosco, when the community's new title became the well-known Salesians of Don (father) Bosco.

THE CHARACTERISTICS OF SALESIAN SPIRITUALITY

As a whole, the following might be considered as the distinguishing emphases of a Jesus-centered Salesian spirituality:

Theological optimism: God's creation, especially the human person (even though it is seriously flawed), is good. What God accomplished in creation—good (six days) and very good (seventh day)—was not able to be undone by human sin. We have the God-given power within us to respond to God's love. The image of God is primarily that of Divine Lover. All beauty is a glimpse of God. Choosing the positive interpretation over the negative.

Respect for the Human Person in every circumstance, no matter their status, condition, or religion. All are brothers and sisters—solidarity with all humans and, in fact, with all creation in the diverse universe. Francis describes creation as a united diversity, and a diverse unity that he coins as *unidiversity*.

The Mystery of the Will of God:
a. God's expressed will: all creation was willed by God. Much can be known of God's will by knowing yourself, the commandments, the counsels of Jesus, and the guidance of the Church, so that we can make free decisions that become the will of God for us.

b. God's allowed will: God permeates and saturates all existence with his presence, allowing the universe the freedom to use his creative energy as it does, and embrace whatever may happen within his Loving Care.

c. Embracing God's will: Accepting the present moment in any eventuality as an opportunity to respond according to God's grace, and uniting ourselves completely with the will of God, so that our will becomes his and his will becomes ours.

Devotion and Holiness: We can each be devout and holy according to the virtues called for in our differing lives, amidst great busyness and many personal relationships.

Holiness is not limited to priests and sisters. We are all called to "Live Jesus."

Prayer: Living with mindfulness of God's presence, doing all for the love of God, uniting our heart with that of the Divine Lover, and coordinating the rhythm of hearts beating together. Prayer is needed power for the spiritual life.

Freedom: Gloriously free to respond to our salvation in Jesus, to create our own mindset and response, and free to pray as the Spirit moves us.

Indifference: Apart from attachment to God, everything else is peripheral, even success; thy will be done; maintaining peace and calm in all circumstances. Complete union with the will of God in each moment with equanimity.

Interior Life of the Heart: The very center of the person and the locus of holy growth is the heart; always a preference for the interior rather than the exterior, and winning hearts by living Jesus. Prayer is heart to heart with God. Preaching is to reach hearts. "Lips speak to ears, but heart speaks to heart."

Littleness: Preference for the little virtues, the things of everyday actions: humility, cheerfulness, gentleness, kindness, thoughtfulness, patience, sweetness of heart, poverty of spirit, simplicity of life, caring for one another, bearing with one another, and forgiving each other, all with tranquility, not overeagerness. Our holiness ought to be attractive to others, rather than a burden for them to endure.

Francis de Sales, more than any other Doctor of the Church, has had an influence on today's understanding of God and the call to holiness for all people to live by the Spirit and bring Christ to the world, or in his words, "Live Jesus."

Select Bibliography

Boenzi, Joseph. *Saint Francis de Sales: Life and Spirit*. Stella Niagara, NY: DeSales Resource Center, 2013.

De Sales, Francis. *Francis de Sales, Jane de Chantal: Letters of Spiritual Direction*, The Classics of Western Spirituality. Translated by Peronne Marie Thibert, VHM. Selected and Introduced by Wendy M. Wright and Joseph Power, OSFS, Preface by Henri J.M. Nouwen. New York: Paulist Press, 1988.

———. *Introduction to the Devout Life*. Translated and edited by John K. Ryan. New York: Image Books/Doubleday, 2003.

———. *St. Francis de Sales: Selected Letters*. Translated by Elizabeth Stopp. Stella Niagara, NY: DeSales Resource Center, 2011.

———. *Thy Will Be Done: Fifty-Eight Letters to Souls Troubles That Afflict Each of Us Today*. Manchester, NH: Sophia Institute Press, 1995.

———. *Treatise On the Love of God*. Translated by John K. Ryan. 2 vols. Stella Niagara, NY: DeSales Resource Center, 2007.

Duhigg, Charles. *The Power of Habit: Why We Do What We Do and How to Change*. London: Random House, 2012.

Hanson, Rick. *Just One Thing: Developing a Buddha Brain One Simple Practice at a Time*. Oakland, CA: New Harbinger Publications, 2011.

Harris, Russ. *The Reality Slap: Finding Peace and Fulfillment when Life Hurts*. Oakland, CA: New Harbinger Publications, 2012.

McDonnell, Eunan. *God Desires You: St. Francis de Sales on Living the Gospel*. Stella Niagara, NY: DeSales Resource Center, 2008.

Ravier, André. *Francis de Sales, Sage and Saint*. Translated by Joseph D. Bowler, OSFS. Rev. ed. Stella Niagara, NY: DeSales Resource Center, 2007.

———. *Saint Jeanne de Chantal: Noble Lady, Holy Woman*. Translated by Mary Emily Hamilton. Stella Niagara, NY: DeSales Resource Center, 2007.

For more information and resources on Salesian books and spirituality, visit the Web site: www.EmbracedbyGod.org.